I0213393

SRIMAD BHAGAVAD GITA

SRIMAD BHAGAVAD GITA

English Translation and Commentary by

SWAMI SWARUPANANDA

[1909]

WWW.ANDRASNAGY.ORG

ISBN: 978-1-968194-10-9

Contents

Characters

Arjuna The third Pandava prince and the central human figure in the Gita. A great warrior and archer who faces a moral and emotional crisis on the battlefield of Kurukshetra.

Krishna An incarnation of Lord Vishnu and Arjuna's charioteer, guide, and divine teacher. Krishna delivers the teachings of the Bhagavad Gita.

Sanjaya The narrator of the Gita. He is King Dhritarashtra's advisor and is granted divine vision to describe the events of the battlefield.

Dhritarashtra The blind king of the Kauravas and father of Duryodhana. Although not physically present in the battlefield, he listens to the narration of the war and the Gita from Sanjaya.

Duryodhana The eldest of the Kauravas and Arjuna's cousin. He is a key antagonist in the Mahabharata war. Though not a speaker in the Gita, his ambition sets the stage for the battle.

Bhishma Grand-uncle of both Pandavas and Kauravas. Commander of the Kaurava army. Revered for his vow of celibacy and loyalty.

Drona Royal guru of both the Pandavas and Kauravas. Fights on the side of the Kauravas.

Karna A great warrior allied with the Kauravas. Half-brother of the Pandavas, though this is not known to most during the war.

Yudhishthira Eldest of the Pandava brothers, known for his righteousness.

Bhima The second Pandava, known for his immense strength.

Nakula & Sahadeva Twin Pandava brothers, skilled in swordsmanship and knowledge, respectively.

Kritavarma, Shalya, Ashwatthama, etc. Other warriors mentioned during the descriptions of the battle formations and key moments.

FOREWORD

The Srimad Bhagavad Gitâ occurs in the Bhishma Parva of the Mahâbhârata and comprises 18 chapters from the 25th to the 42nd. The discourse between Arjuna and Krishna on the battle-field, on the eve of the war which forms the subject-matter of the work, was strung together in seven hundred verses and put in its place in the body of his great history by Vyâsa.

The Gitâ opens with Dhritarâshtra's query to Sanjaya about the progress of events. In the second chapter of the Bhishma Parva, we find Vyâsa offering the power of sight to the blind king, that he might see the war. Dhritarâshtra declined to have it, saying he did not care to have eyes with which only to see the death of his own people; but he would like to hear what was happening. On this the great Rishi Vyâsa said, that all the occurrences in connection with the war would be reflected in the mind of Sanjaya, and he would faithfully report them to Dhritarâshtra.

The Gitâ is called an Upanishad, because it contains the essence of Self-knowledge, and because its teachings, like those of the Vedas, are divided into three sections, Karma (work), Upâsanâ (devotion) and Jnâna (knowledge).

The first chapter is introductory. The second is a summary of the whole work, e.g., in II. 48 and the connected Slokas, self-less work devoid of desire for fruits, is taught for the purification of the heart; in II. 61 and the connected Slokas devotion is taught to the pure-hearted, to qualify them further for the highest Sannyâsa, which last is taught in II. 71 and the connected Slokas.

It is also usual to divide the work into three sections illustrative of the three terms of the Mahâvâkya of the Sâma-Veda, "Thou art That" (Chhând. Upa., VI. viii. 7). In this view the first six chapters explain the path of work without desire for fruits, and the nature of "Thou." The next six chapters deal with devotion and the nature of "That." The last six describe the state of the highest knowledge and the nature of the middle term of the Mahâvâkya, in other words, the means of re-establishing the identity of "Thou" and "That."

The central teaching of the Gitâ is the attainment of Freedom, by the performance of one's Swadharma or duty in life. "Do thy duty without an eye to the results thereof. Thus shouldst thou gain the purification of heart which is essential for Moksha,"—seems to be the keynote of Krishna's teachings to Arjuna.

It is well known why the Gitâ came into existence. It was owing to Arjuna's unwillingness to do his duty as a Kshatriya—to fight for a just cause—because it involved the destruction of his own people. Not that Arjuna did not recognise the justice and right of the cause, but he would rather renounce the world and try for Moksha than kill his relatives and friends. Krishna's characterisation of this weakly sentimental attitude of Arjuna is well known. He called it "Un-Arya-like delusion, contrary to the attainment alike of heaven and honour" and exhorted Pârtha to "yield not to unmanliness" but to "cast off this mean faintheartedness." (II. 2-3). "Could a coward who fails to do his duty, be worthy to attain Moksha?"—seems to be Krishna's rejoinder. Could a man not purified by the fire-ordeal of his Swadharma, could a renegade, a slave, attain Moksha? No! says the Lord. And this is the lesson we Indians have forgotten all these years, though we have been reading and discussing the Gitâ all the time.

S.

MEDITATION

1. Om! O Bhagavad Gitâ, with which Pârtha was enlightened by the Lord Nârâyana Himself and which was incorporated in the Mahâbhârata by the ancient sage Vyâsa,—the Blessed Mother, the Destroyer of rebirth, showering down the nectar of Advaita, and consisting of eighteen chapters,—upon Thee, O Bhagavad Gitâ! O Loving Mother! I meditate.

2. Salutation to thee, O Vyâsa, of mighty intellect and with eyes large like the petals of full-blown lotuses, by whom was lighted the lamp of wisdom, full of the Mahâbhârata-oil.

3. Salutation to Krishna, the holder of the Jnânamudrâ, granter of desires of those who take refuge in Him, the milker of the Gitâ-nectar, in whose hand is the cane for driving cows.

4. All the Upanishads are the cows, the Son of the cowherd is the milker, Pârtha is the calf, men of purified intellect are the drinkers and the supreme nectar Gitâ is the milk.

5. I salute Krishna, the Guru of the Universe, God, the son of Vasudeva, the Destroyer of Karma and Chânura, the supreme bliss of Devaki.

6. The battle-river, with Bhishma and Drona as its banks, and Jayadratha as the water, with the king of Gândhâra as the blue water-lily, and Shalya as the shark, with Kripa as the current and

Karna as the breakers, with Ashvatthâmâ and Vikarna as terrible Makaras and Duryodhana as the whirlpool in it,—was indeed crossed over by the Pândavas, with Keshava as the ferry-man.

7. May the taintless lotus of the Mahâbhârata, growing on the waters of the words of Parâshara's son, having the

Gitâ as its strong sweet fragrance, with many a narrative as its stamens, fully opened by the discourses on Hari and drunk joyously day after day by the Bhramara of the good and the pure in the world,—be productive of the supreme good to him who is eager to destroy the taint of Kali!

8. I salute that All-bliss Mâdhava whose compassion makes the mute eloquent and the cripple cross mountains.

9. Salutation to that God Whom the creator Brahmâ, Varuna, Indra, Rudra and the Maruts praise with divine hymns; Whom the singers of Sâma sing, by the Vedas, with their full complement of parts, consecutive sections and Upanishads; Whom the Yogis see with their minds absorbed in Him through perfection in meditation, and Whose limit the hosts of Devas and Asuras know not.

INVOCATION[1]

O blessed Mother
Who showerest (upon us) the nectar of Advaita
In the form of (these) eighteen chapters!
Thou Destroyer of rebirth!
Thou loving Mother!
Thou Bhagavad Gitâ!
Upon Thee I meditate.

Thee, O Vyâsa, of lotus-eyes,
And mighty intellect,
Who hast lighted the lamp of wisdom
Filled with the oil of the Mahâbhârata,
Thee we salute.

O Thou who art the Refuge
Of the (ocean-born) Lakshmi,
Thou in whose right hand is the shepherd's crook,
Who art the milker of the divine nectar of the Gitâ,
To Thee, O Krishna, to Thee our salutation!

The Upanishads are even as the herd of cows,
The Son of the cowherd as the milker,
Pârtha as the sucking-calf,
And men of purified intellect the drinkers,
Of this, the supreme nectar, the milk of the Gitâ.

Thou son of Vasudeva,
Destroyer of Kamsa and Chânura,
Thou supreme bliss of Devaki,
Guru of the Worlds,
Thee, O Krishna, as God, we salute!

Of that great river of battle which the Pândavas crossed over,
Bhishma and Drona were as the high banks;
And Jayadratha as the water of the river;
The King of Gândhâra the water-lily;
Shalya as the sharks, Kripa as the current;
Karna the mighty waves;
Ashvatthâmâ and Vikarna dread water-monsters,

1 Another rendering of the "Meditation."

And Duryodhana was the very whirlpool;
 But Thou, O Krishna, wast the Ferry-man!

This spotless product of the words of Vyâsa,
This lotus of the Mahâbhârata,—
With the Bhagavad Gitâ as its strong sweet fragrance,
And tales of heroes as its full-blown petals,
Held ever open by the talk of Hari, of Him
Who is destroyer of the taint of Kali-Yuga;
This lotus to which come joyously
Day after day the honey-seeking souls,—
 May this produce in us the highest good!

Him Whose compassion maketh the dumb man eloquent,
And the cripple to cross mountains,
Him the All-blissful Mâdhava,
 Do I salute!

To that Supreme One Who is bodied forth in Brahmâ,
In Varuna, in Indra, in Rudra and Maruts;
That One Whom all divine beings praise with hymns;
Him Whom the singers of Sâma-Veda tell;
Him of Whose glory, sing in full choir, The Upanishads and Vedas;
Him Whom the Yogis see, with mind absorbed in perfect meditation;
Him of Whom all the hosts of Devas and Asuras
Know not the limitations,
To Him, the Supreme Good, be salutation,—
Him we salute. Him we salute. Him we salute.

FIRST CHAPTER
The Grief of Arjuna

Dhritarâshtra said:

1. Tell me, O Sanjaya! Assembled on Kurukshetra, the centre of religious activity, desirous to fight, what indeed did my people and the Pândavas do? [2]

Sanjaya said:

2. But then King Duryodhana, having seen the Pândava forces in battle-array, approached his teacher Drona, and spoke these words: [3]

3. "Behold, O Teacher! this mighty army of the sons of Pându, arrayed by the son of Drupada, thy gifted pupil. [4]

4-6. "Here (are) heroes, mighty archers, the equals in battle of Bhima and Arjuna—the great warriors Yuyudhâna, Virâta, Drupada; the valiant Dhrishtaketu, Chekitâna and the king of Kâshi; the best of men, Purujit, Kunti-Bhoja and Shaivya; the powerful Yudhâmanyu, and the brave Uttamaujas, the son of Subhadrâ, and the sons of Draupadi,—lords of great chariots.[5]

7. "Hear also, O Best of the twice-born! the names of those who (are) distinguished amongst ourselves, the leaders of my army. These I relate

---

2 True it is that the two parties were gathered together for battle, but was the influence of Kurukshetra, the sacred centre of religious and spiritual activity from of old, barren of any result? Did not the spiritual influence of the spot affect any of the leaders in a way unfavourable to the occurrence of the battle? is the purport of Dhritarâshtra's question.

3 Sanjaya's reply beginning with "But then" and describing Duryodhana's action is a plain hint to the old king that his son was afraid. For he went to his teacher (regarded as father) instead of to the commander-in-chief, as a child in fright would run to its parents in preference to others.

4 As a scorpion would sting even that whose protection is sought to be free from fear, so did the wicked Duryodhana insult his teacher. His meaning in plain words comes to this: just think of your stupidity in teaching the science of fight to the son of Drupada and to those of Pându. They are now arrayed to kill you!

5 great-charioted: one who is well-versed in the science of war and commands eleven thousand bowmen.

(to you) for your information.[6]

8. "Yourself and Bhishma and Karna and Kripa, the victorious in war. Asvatthâmâ and Vikarna and Jayadratha, the son of Somadatta.[7]

9. "And many other heroes also, well-skilled in fight, and armed with many kinds of weapons, are here, determined to lay down their lives for my sake.

10. "This our army defended by Bhishma (is) impossible to be counted, but that army of theirs, defended by Bhima (is) easy to number.[8]

11. "(Now) do, being stationed in your proper places in the divisions of the army, support Bhishma alone."[9]

12. That powerful, oldest of the Kurus, Bhishma the grandsire, in order to cheer Duryodhana, now sounded aloud a lion-roar and blew his conch.[10]

13. Then following Bhishma, conches and kettle-drums, tabors, trumpets and cowhorns blared forth suddenly from the Kaurava side and the noise was tremendous.

6 However well-versed in the science of war you might be, you are after all a Brâhmana (best of the twice-born) a lover of peace, that is to say, a coward. It is therefore natural for you to be afraid of the Pândava force. But take heart, we too have, great warriors in our ranks—is the veiled meaning of Duryodhana's words.

7 Afraid lest he had said too much Duryodhana is flattering Drona, by mentioning the latter before even Bhishma and qualifying Drona's brother-in law with the phrase 'victorious in war,' a move likely to touch the heart of most mortals.

8 In ancient Indian warfare, one commanding a force had for his main-stay a defender about him, whose position was no less important. Here are given the names of the chief defenders, and not of the chief commanders.

9 Since I cannot expect from you any initiative, do what you are told to do,—seems to be Duryodhana's intention.

10 All eyes were turned upon Duryodhana and the penetrating intelligence of Bhishma detected his fear; and since Drona took no notice of Duryodhana's words, knowing his grandson as he did, he had no difficulty in understanding that the latter had spoken to his teacher in a way which called forth Drona's coldness instead of his enthusiasm. The grandsire's heart was moved with pity and hence the action on his part described in the above verse. It should here be noted that this action, amounting to a challenge, really began the fight. It was the Kaurava side again which took the aggressor's part.

14. Then, also, Mâdhava and Pândava, stationed in their magnificent chariot yoked with white horses, blew their divine conches with a furious noise.

15. Hrishikesha blew the Pânchajanya, Dhananjaya, the Devadatta, and Vrikodara, the doer of terrific deeds, his large conch Paundra.

16. King Yudhishthira, son of Kunti, blew the conch named Anantavijaya, and Nakula and Sahadeva, their Sughosha and Manipushpaka.

17. The expert bowman, king of Kâshi, and the great warrior Shikhandi, Dhrishtadyumna and Virâta and the unconquered Sâtyaki;

18. O Lord of Earth! Drupada and the sons of Draupadi, and the mighty-armed son of Subhadrâ, all, also blew each his own conch.

19. And the terrific noise resounding throughout heaven and earth rent the hearts of Dhritarâshtra's party.[11]

20. Then, O Lord of Earth, seeing Dhritarâshtra's party standing marshalled and the shooting about to begin, that Pândava whose ensign was the monkey, raising his bow, said the following words to Krishna:[12]

Arjuna said:

21-22. Place my chariot, O Achyuta! between the two armies that I may see those who stand here prepared for war. On this eve of battle (let me know) with whom I have to fight.

23. For I desire to observe those who are assembled here for fight, wishing to please the evil-minded Duryodhana by taking his side on this

11 Verses 14-19 are full of hints about the superiority of the Pândava party and the consequent sure defeat of Dhritarâshtra. The figure to which Sanjaya draws the old king's attention as first taking up Bhishma's challenge, is described by him as the Lord of Fortune and the Pândava—the best of the Pându princes. Note also the details in which the chariot, horses and conches of the Pândava party are described, and finally though the army of the Kauravas was more than a third as much again as that of the Pândavas, the noise made by the former was only tremendous, whereas that of the latter was not only tremendous but filled the earth and sky with reverberations and rent the hearts of the former.

12 In view of the sudden change of feeling that is to come over Arjuna it should be noted how full of the war-spirit we find him in this verse.

battle-field.[13]

Sanjaya said:

24-25. Commanded thus by Gudâkesha, Hrishikesha, O Bhârata, drove that grandest of chariots to a place between the two hosts, facing Bhishma, Drona and all the rulers of the earth, and then spoke thus, "Behold, O Pârtha, all the Kurus gathered together!"

26. Then saw Pârtha stationed there in both the armies, grandfathers, fathers-in-law and uncles, brothers and cousins, his own and their sons and grandsons, and comrades, teachers, and other friends as well.

27. Then he, the son of Kunti, seeing all those kinsmen stationed in their ranks, spoke thus sorrowfully, filled with deep compassion.

Arjuna said:

29. Seeing, O Krishna, these my kinsmen gathered here, eager for fight, my limbs fail me, and my mouth is parched up. I shiver all over, and my hair stands on end. The bow Gândiva slips from my hand, and my skin burns.[14]

30. Neither, O Keshava, can I stand upright. My mind is in a whirl. And I see adverse omens.

31. Neither, O Krishna, do I see any good in killing these my own people in battle. I desire neither victory nor empire, nor yet pleasure.

32-34. Of what avail is dominion to us, of what avail are pleasures and even life, if these, O Govinda! for whose sake it is desired that empire, enjoyment and pleasure should be ours, themselves stand here in battle, having renounced life and wealth—Teachers, uncles, sons and also grandfathers, maternal uncles, fathers-in-law, grandsons, brothers-in-law, besides other kinsmen.

35. Even though these were to kill me, O slayer of Madhu, I could not wish to kill them, not even for the sake of dominion over the three worlds, how much less for the sake of the earth!

---

13 Arjuna is impatient to see who dared face him in fight!

14 Compassion overpowered him. Not that it was due to discrimination, but rather to the lack of this. He lost self-control—the first step into the abyss of ignorance.

36. What pleasure indeed could be ours, O Jnanârdana, from killing these sons of Dhritarâshtra? Sin only could take hold of us by the slaying of these felons.[15]

37. Therefore ought we not to kill our kindred, the sons of Dhritarâshtra. For how could we, O Mâdhava, gain happiness by the slaying of our own kinsmen?

38-39. Though these, with understanding overpowered by greed, see no evil due to decay of families, and no sin in hostility to friends, why should we, O Janârdana, who see clearly the evil due to the decay of families, not turn away from this sin?

40. On the decay of a family the immemorial religious rites of that family die out. On the destruction of spirituality, impiety further overwhelms the whole of the family.

41. On the prevalence of impiety, O Krishna, the women of the family become corrupt; and women being corrupted, there arises, O Vârshneya, intermingling of castes.

42. Admixture of castes, indeed, is for the hell of the family and the destroyers of the family; their ancestors fall, deprived of the offerings of rice-ball and water.[16]

43. By these misdeeds of the destroyers of the family, bringing about confusion of castes, are the immemorial religious rites of the caste and the family destroyed.

15 Felons: Atatâyi, one who sets fire to the house of, administers poison to, falls upon with a sword on, steals the wealth, land and wife of, another person. Duryodhana did all these to the Pândava brothers. According to the Artha Shâstras, no sin is incurred by killing an Atatâyin, even if he be thoroughly versed in Vedânta. But Arjuna seems to argue, "True, there may not be incurred the particular sin of slaying one's own kith and kin by killing the sons of Dhritarâshtra inasmuch as they are Atatâyins, but then the general sin of killing is sure to take hold of us, for Dharma Shâstra which is more authoritative than Artha Shâstra enjoins non-killing."

16 Verily, confusion of family is the hell of destroyers of family. (For then do) their own ancestors fall, deprived &c. This refers to the well-known Srâddha ceremony of the Hindus, the main principle of which consists in sending helpful thoughts to the dead relations, as well as to all the occupants of Pitri-loka (a temporary abode, immediately after death) accompanied with (to make the thoughts more forcible) concrete offerings. The poor are also fed to secure their good wishes.

44. We have heard, O Janârdana, that inevitable is the dwelling in hell of those men in whose families religious practices have been destroyed.

45. Alas, we are involved in a great sin, in that we are prepared to slay our kinsmen, from greed of the pleasures of a kingdom!

46. Verily, if the sons of Dhritarâshtra, weapons in hand, were to slay me, unresisting and unarmed, in the battle, that would be better for me.

Sanjaya said:

47. Speaking thus in the midst of the battle-field, Arjuna casting away his bow and arrows, sank down on the seat of his chariot, with his mind distressed with sorrow.

SECOND CHAPTER
The Way of Knowledge

Sanjaya said:

1. To him who was thus overwhelmed with pity and sorrowing, and whose eyes were dimmed with tears, Madhusudana spoke these words: [17]

The Blessed Lord said:

2. In such a crisis, whence comes upon thee, O Arjuna, this dejection, un-Aryalike, disgraceful and contrary to the attainment of heaven? [18]

3. Yield not to unmanliness, O son of Prithâ! Ill doth it become thee. Cast off this mean faint-heartedness and arise, O scorcher of thine enemies!

Arjuna said:

4. —But how can I, in battle, O slayer of Madhu, fight with arrows

---

17 Overwhelmed with pity: Not Arjuna, but Arjuna's feeling was master of the situation.

18 Mark with what contempt Krishna regards Arjuna's attitude of weakness masked by religious expression!

against Bhishma and Drona, who are rather worthy to be worshipped, O destroyer of foes!

5. Surely it would be better even to eat the bread of beggary in this life than to slay these great-souled masters. But if I kill them, even in this world, all my enjoyment of wealth and desires will be stained with blood. [19]

6. And indeed I can scarcely tell which will be better, that we should conquer them, or that they should conquer us. The very sons of Dhritarâshtra,—after slaying whom we should not care to live,—stand facing us.

7. With my nature overpowered by weak commiseration, with a mind in confusion about duty, I supplicate Thee. Say decidedly what is good for me. I am Thy disciple. Instruct me who have taken refuge in Thee.[20]

8. I do not see anything to remove this sorrow which blasts my senses, even were I to obtain unrivalled and flourishing dominion over the earth, and mastery over the gods.

Sanjaya said:

9. Having spoken thus to the Lord of the senses, Gudâkesha, the scorcher of foes, said to Govinda, "I shall not fight," and became silent. [21]

10. To him who was sorrowing in the midst of the two armies, Hri-

---

19 i.e. even in this world I shall be in hell.

20 Dharma is the ness, the law of the inmost constitution of a thing. The primary meaning of Dharma is not virtue or religion, but that is only its secondary significance. Fighting in a just cause is the religious duty or Dharma of a Kshatriya, while the same is a sin to a Brâhmana, because it is contrary to the law of his being. Working out one's Karma according to the law of one's own being is therefore the Dharma or religion or way to salvation of an individual. The cloud of Karma hides the Self-Sun from view. The means which exhausts this cloud without adding to it and thus helps in one's Self-restoration is one's Dharma.

Thy disciple: Until this declaration has been made, the Master may not give the highest knowledge.

21 The object of Sanjaya in using these names is to remind Dhritarâshtra—who may naturally be a little elated at the prospect of Arjuna's not fighting —that this is only a temporary weakness, since by the presence of the Lord of the senses all ignorance must eventually be dispelled. Arjuna's own nature also is devoid of darkness. Is he not the conqueror of sleep, and the terror of foes?

shikesha, as if smiling, O descendant of Bharata! spoke these words.[22]

The Blessed Lord said:

11. Thou hast been mourning for them who should not be mourned for. Yet thou speakest words of wisdom. The (truly) wise grieve neither for the living nor the dead.[23]

12. It is not that I have never existed, nor thou, nor these kings. Nor is it that we shall cease to exist in the future.[24]

13. As are childhood, youth, and old age, in this body, to the embodied soul, so also is the attaining of another body. Calm souls are not deluded thereat.[25]

14. Notions of heat and cold, of pain and pleasure, are born, O son of Kunti, only of the contact of the senses with their objects. They have a beginning and an end. They are impermanent in their nature. Bear them patiently, O descendant of Bharata.[26]

15. That calm man who is the same in pain and pleasure, whom these cannot disturb, alone is able, O great amongst men, to attain to immortality.[27]

---

22 Smiling—to drown Arjuna in the ocean of shame. Krishna's smile at Arjuna's sorrow is like the lightning that plays over the black monsoon cloud. The rain bursts forth, and the thirsty earth is saturated. It is the smile of the coming illumination.

23 Words of wisdom: Vide I. 35-44.

24 Of course Krishna here does not mean that the body is immortal, but refers to the true Self, behind all bodies.

25 According to this, the continuity of the ego is no more interrupted by death than by the passing of childhood into youth and youth into old age in this body.

Calm souls: Those who have become calm by Self-realisation.

26 They have a beginning and an end: as distinguished from the Permanent Self. The more one is able to identify oneself with the Permanent Self, the less one is affected by the agreeable and disagreeable conditions of life.

Impermanent in their nature: That is, the same object which gives pleasure at one moment gives pain at another, and so on.

27 Thus perfect sameness amidst the ills of life means full and unbroken consciousness of our oneness with the Immortal Self. Thus is immortality attained.

16. The unreal never is. The Real never is not. Men possessed of the knowledge of the Truth fully know both these.[28]

17. That by which all this is pervaded,—That know for certain to be indestructible. None has the power to destroy this Immutable.[29]

18. Of this indwelling Self, the ever-changeless, the indestructible, the illimitable,—these bodies are said to have an end. Fight therefore, O descendant of Bharata.[30]

19. He who takes the Self to be the slayer, he who takes It to be the slain, neither of these knows. It does not slay, nor is It slain.[31]

20. This in never born, nor does It die. It is not that not having been It again comes into being. (Or according to another view: It is not that having been It again ceases to be). This is unborn, eternal, changeless, ever-Itself. It is not killed when the body is killed.[32]

21. He that knows This to be indestructible, changeless, without birth, and immutable, how is he, O son of Prithâ, to slay or cause another to slay? [33]

22. Even as a man casts off worn-out clothes, and puts on others which are new, so the embodied casts off worn-out bodies, and enters into others which are new.[34]

---

28 Unreal: Real: The determination of the nature of the Real is the quest of all philosophy. Sri Krishna here states that a thing which never remains the same for any given period is unreal, and that the Real on the other hand is always the same. The whole of the phenomenal world, therefore, must be unreal, because in it no one state endures for even an infinitesimal division of time. And that which takes note of this incessant change, and is therefore itself changeless,—the Atman, Consciousness,—is the Real.

29 That by which all this is pervaded, i.e. He that pervades all this as the Witness.

30 Arjuna's grief which deters him from his duty of fighting against the Kauravas is born of ignorance as to the true nature of the Soul. Hence Sri Bhagavân's strong and repeated attempts to illumine him on the subject.

31 Cf. Katha Up. I. ii. 19-20.

32 This sloka refers in the sense of denial to the six kinds of modification inherent in matter: birth, subsistence, growth, transformation, decay, and death.

33 How is he to slay?—referring to Arjuna. To cause another to slay—referring to Krishna's own part.

34 As one only puts off the old, when one already possesses the new garment, so the embodied is already entering a new body in the act of leaving

23. This (Self), weapons cut not; This, fire burns not; This, water wets not; and This, wind dries not.

24. This Self cannot be cut, nor burnt, nor wetted, nor dried. Changeless, all-pervading, unmoving, immovable, the Self is eternal.

25. This (Self) is said to be unmanifested, unthinkable, and unchangeable. Therefore, knowing This to be such, thou oughtest not to mourn.[35]

26. But if thou shouldst take This to have constant birth and death, even in that case, O mighty-armed, thou oughtest not to mourn for This. [36]

27. Of that which is born, death is certain, of that which is dead, birth is certain. Over the unavoidable, therefore, thou oughtest not to grieve. [37]

28. All beings are unmanifested in their beginning, O Bhârata, manifested in their middle state and unmanifested again in their end. What is there then to grieve about?[38]

29. Some look upon the Self as marvellous. Others speak of It as wonderful. Others again hear of It as a wonder. And still others, though hearing, do not understand It at all.[39]

---

this. The Upanishad compares this to the movement of a leech, which has already established a new foothold before leaving the old.

35 This Self is infinite and partless, so can be neither subject nor object of any action.

36 Krishna here, for the sake of argument, takes up the materialistic supposition, and shows that even if the Self were impermanent, sorrow ought to be destroyed, since in that case there would be no hereafter, no sin, and no hell.

37 This sloka concerns only those who are not yet free. So long as there is desire, birth and death are inevitable.
Therefore thou oughtest not to grieve: Since you cannot control the inevitable and preserve the bodies of your relations, work out your own Karma and go beyond both birth and death.

38 Beings: In their relationships as sons and friends, who are mere combinations of material elements, correlated as causes and effects.
The idea here is that that which has no existence in the beginning and in the end, must be merely illusory in the interim, and should not therefore be allowed to have any influence upon the mind.

39 The sloka may also be interpreted in the sense that those who see, hear and speak of the Self are wonderful men, because their number is so small. It is not therefore remarkable that you should mourn, because the Atman

30. This, the Indweller in the bodies of all, is ever indestructible, O descendant of Bharata. Wherefore thou oughtest not to mourn for any creature.[40]

31. Looking at thine own Dharma, also, thou oughtest not to waver, for there is nothing higher for a Kshatriya than a righteous war.[41]

32. Fortunate certainly are the Kshatriyas, O son of Prithâ, who are called to fight in such a battle, that comes unsought as an open gate to heaven.[42]

33. But if thou refusest to engage in this righteous warfare, then, forfeiting thine own Dharma and honour, thou shalt incur sin.

34. The world also will ever hold thee in reprobation. To the honoured, disrepute is surely worse than death.[43]

35. The great chariot-warriors[44] will believe that thou hast withdrawn from the battle through fear. And thou wilt be lightly esteemed by them who have thought much of thee.

36. Thine enemies also, cavilling at thy great prowess, will say of thee things that are not to be uttered. What could be more intolerable than this?

37. Dying thou gainest heaven; conquering thou enjoyest the earth. Therefore, O son of Kunti, arise, resolved to fight.

38. Having made pain and pleasure, gain and loss, conquest and defeat, the same, engage thou then in battle. So shalt thou incur no sin.[45]

---

is so difficult to comprehend.

40 Krishna here returns to His own point of view.

41 That is to say, it is the duty of a Kshatriya to fight in the interest of his country, people and religion.

42 The Shâstras say that if a Kshatriya fighting for a righteous cause falls in the battle-field, he at once go to heaven.

43 The present argument,—slokas 33-36, assumes that the cause in hand is already proved to be right. Hence it could only be from cowardice that Arjuna could abandon it. Even a hero may be weakened by the stirring of his deepest emotions.

44 Vide commentary I. 6.

45 It is always the desire for one of the pairs of opposites that binds. When an act is done without attachment either for itself or its fruit, then Karma can be worked out without adding to its store, and this leads to Freedom.

39. The wisdom of Self-realisation has been declared unto thee. Hearken thou now to the wisdom of Yoga, endued with which, O son of Prithâ, thou shalt break through the bonds of Karma.[46]

40. In this, there is no waste of the unfinished attempt, nor is there production of contrary results. Even very little of this Dharma protects from the great terror.[47]

41. In this, O scion of Kuru, there is but a single one-pointed determination. The purposes of the undecided are innumerable and many-branching.[48]

42-44. O Pârtha, no set determination is formed in the minds of those that are deeply attached to pleasure and power, and whose discrimination is stolen away by the flowery words of the unwise, who are full of desires and look upon heaven as their highest goal and who, taking pleasure in the panegyric words of the Vedas, declare that there is nothing else. Their (flowery) words are exuberant with various specific, rites as the means

46 Yoga:—Karma Yoga, or that plan of conduct which secures the working out of past Karma; non-accumulation of new; and the striving for Self-realisation with the whole of the will. In this discipline, one's sole object in life is Self-realisation; hence no importance is attached to anything else. Thus all actions are performed without attachment, or care for results. So no new Karma is made: only the already accumulated is exhausted. And at the same time, the whole will is left free to devote itself to the achievement of Self-realisation alone.

In the preceding slokas, 11-25, Krishna has given the point of view of the highest knowledge, the ancient Brahmajnâna. In the 25th and 27th we have a purely materialistic standpoint. Slokas 28 to 37 give the attitude of a man of the world. In the 38th we have an anticipation of the Yoga. And in what is to follow, we have Sri Krishna's own contribution to the philosophy of life.

47 Waste of the unfinished attempt: A religious rite or ceremony performed for a definite object, if left uncompleted, is wasted, like a house unroofed which is neither serviceable nor enduring. In Karma Yoga, however, that is, action and worship performed without desire, this law does not apply, for every effort results in immediate purification of the heart. Production of contrary results: In worship for an object, any imperfection in the process produces positive loss instead of gain. As in cases of sickness, the non-use of the right medicine results in death. The great terror: Being caught in the wheel of birth and death.

48 In Karma Yoga, the one goal is Self-realisation. The undecided (that is, about the highest), naturally devote themselves to lower ideals, no one of which can satisfy. Thus they pass from plan to plan.

to pleasure and power and are the causes of (new) births as the result of their works (performed with desire).[49]

45. The Vedas deal with the three Gunas. Be thou free, O Arjuna, from the triad of the Gunas, free from the pairs of opposites, ever-balanced, free from (the thought of) getting and keeping, and established in the Self.[50]

46. To the Brâhmana who has known the Self, all the Vedas are of so much use as a reservoir is, when there is a flood everywhere.[51]

47. Thy right is to work only; but never to the fruits thereof. Be thou not the producer of the fruits of (thy) actions; neither let thy attachment be towards inaction.[52]

---

49 Samâdhi has been rendered into 'mind' in the above. The generally accepted significance of the term (absorption in God-consciousness produced by deep meditation) would give an equally consistent and happy meaning: Persons attached to pleasure and power cannot have perfect steadiness of mind in divine meditation.
Panegyric words of the Vedas: The Karma Kânda or the sacrificial portion of the Vedas which lays down specific rules for specific actions and their fruits, and extols these latter unduly. Nothing else: Beyond the heavenly enjoyments procurable by the sacrificial rites of the Vedas.

50 The Vedas deal with etc.: That is to say, the Vedas treat of relativity.
Pairs of opposites: Dvandva, all correlated ideas and sensations, e.g., good and bad, pleasure and pain, heat and cold, light and darkness, etc.

Guna is a technical term of the Sânkhya philosophy: also used in the same sense by the Vedânta. Prakriti or Nature is constituted of three Gunas; Sattva (equilibrium), Rajas (attraction), Tamas (inertia). Prakriti is the three Gunas, not that she has them. Guna is wrongly translated as quality; it is substance as well as quality, matter and force. Wherever there is name and form, there is Guna. Guna also means a rope, that which binds.

51 A man possessed of Self-knowledge has no need whatever of the Vedas. This does not, however, mean that the Vedas are useless; only to the knower of Brahman they have no value, as the transient pleasures derivable from them are comprehended in the infinite bliss of Self-knowledge.

52 Be thou not the producer, etc.: That is, do not work with any desire for results, for actions produce fruits or bondage only if they are performed with desire.
Karma primarily means action, but a much profounder meaning has come to be attached to this word. It means the destiny forged by one in one's past incarnation or present: the store of tendencies, impulses, characteristics, and habits laid by, which determines the future embodiment, environment and the whole of one's organisation.

48. Being steadfast in Yoga, Dhananjaya, perform actions, abandoning attachment, remaining unconcerned as regards success and failure. This evenness of mind (in regard to success and failure) is known as Yoga.

49. Work (with desire) is verily far inferior to that performed with the mind undisturbed by thoughts of results. O Dhananjaya, seek refuge in this evenness of mind. Wretched are they who act for results.

50. Endued with this evenness of mind, one frees oneself in this life, alike from vice and virtue. Devote thyself, therefore, to this Yoga. Yoga is the very dexterity of work.[53]

51. The wise, possessed of this evenness of mind, abandoning the fruits of their actions, freed for ever from the fetters of birth, go to that state which is beyond all evil.

52. When thy intellect crosses beyond the taint of illusion, then shalt thou attain to indifference, regarding things heard and things yet to be heard.[54]

53. When thy intellect, tossed about by the conflict of opinions—has become immovable and firmly established in the Self, then thou shalt attain Self-realisation.

Arjuna said:

54. What, O Keshava, is the description of the man of steady wisdom, merged in Samâdhi? How (on the other hand) does the man of steady wisdom speak, how sit, how walk?[55]

Another meaning of Karma often used in reference to one's caste or position in life, is duty, the course of conduct which one ought to follow in pursuance of the tendencies which one acquired in one's past, with a view to work them out and regain the pristine purity of the Self.

53 Alike from vice and virtue: A follower of Karma Yoga can have no personal motive for any action. Our action without motive becomes colourless, loses its character of vice or virtue.

Dexterity of work: It is the nature of work to produce bondage. Karma Yoga is the dexterity of work because it not only robs work of its power to bind, but also transforms it into an efficient means of freedom.

54 The taint of illusion: the identifying of the Self with the non-Self, the ego.

55 Arjuna is asking, (1) what is the state of the mind of the man of realisation when in Samâdhi? and (2) how is its influence shown in his conduct

The Blessed Lord said:

55. When a man completely casts away, O Pârtha, all the desires of the mind, satisfied in the Self alone by the Self, then is he said to be one of steady wisdom.[56]

56. He whose mind is not shaken by adversity, who does not hanker after happiness, who has become free from affection, fear, and wrath, is indeed the Muni of steady wisdom.[57]

57. He who is everywhere unattached, not pleased at receiving good, nor vexed at evil, his wisdom is fixed.[58]

58. When also, like the tortoise its limbs, he can completely withdraw the senses from their objects, then his wisdom becomes steady.[59]

59. Objects fall away from the abstinent man, leaving the longing behind. But his longing also ceases, who sees the Supreme.[60]

60. The turbulent senses, O son of Kunti, do violently snatch away the mind of even a wise man, striving after perfection.

61. The steadfast, having controlled them all, sits focussed on Me as the Supreme. His wisdom is steady, whose senses are under control.

62. Thinking of objects, attachment to them is formed in a man. From

---

when out of it?

Steady wisdom: Settled conviction of one's identity with Brahman gained by direct realisation.

56 This answers the first part of Arjuna's question.

57 This and the following two slokas answer the second part of Arjuna's question, as to the conduct of one of perfect realisation.

Muni: Man of meditation.

58 Not pleased etc.: consequently he does not praise or blame. This is an answer to the query: "How does he speak?"

59 Withdraw the senses: bring the mind back upon the Self from all sense-objects. This is known as Pratyâhâra in Yoga.

To explain the sloka more fully: a man of the highest realisation can, at any moment, shake himself clear of all impressions of the sense-world and go into Samâdhi, with the ease and naturalness of a tortoise drawing its limbs within itself.

60 Abstinent man: An unillumined person abstaining from sense-pleasure for penance, or because of physical incapacity.

attachment longing, and from longing anger grows.

63. From anger comes delusion, and from delusion loss of memory. From loss of memory comes the ruin of discrimination, and from the ruin of discrimination he perishes.[61]

64. But the self-controlled man, moving among objects with senses under restraint, and free from attraction and aversion, attains to tranquillity.[62]

65. In tranquillity, all sorrow is destroyed. For the intellect of him who is tranquil-minded, is soon established in firmness.[63]

66. No knowledge (of the Self) has the unsteady. Nor has he meditation. To the unmeditative there is no peace. And how can one without peace have happiness?

67. For, the mind which follows in the wake of the wandering senses, carries away his discrimination, as a wind (carries away from its course) a boat on the waters.

68. Therefore, O mighty-armed, his knowledge is steady, whose senses are completely restrained from their objects.[64]

69. That which is night to all beings, in that the self-controlled man wakes. That in which all beings wake, is night to the Self-seeing Muni.[65]

61 A beautiful image appears. The tendency of the mind is to repeat it. Then, if the image is allowed to recur, a liking grows. With the growth of liking the wish to come close, to possess, appears. Any obstacle to this produces wrath. The impulse of anger throws the mind into confusion, which casts a veil over the lessons of wisdom learnt by past experience. Thus deprived of his moral standard, he is prevented from using his discrimination. Failing in discrimination, he acts irrationally, on the impulse of passion, and paves the way to moral death.
Thus Krishna traces moral degradation to those first breaths of thought, that come softly and almost unconsciously to the mind.

62 The above is in answer to Arjuna's fourth question, "How does he move?"

63 That is, firmly concentrates itself on the Self.

64 This does not mean that the senses remain completely estranged, but that they are all estrange-able at will.

65 Where all beings are in darkness, there the Muni sees, and vice versa. The consciousness of the man of realisation is so full of God that he cannot see anything apart from Him. The ignorant man, on the other hand, lives in the

70. As into the ocean,—brimful, and still,—flow the waters, even so the Muni into whom enter all desires, he, and not the desirer of desires, attains to peace.[66]

71. That man who lives devoid of longing, abandoning all desires, without the sense of 'I' and 'mine,' he attains to peace.[67]

72. This is to have one's being in Brahman, O son of Prithâ. None, attaining to this, becomes deluded. Being established therein, even at the end of life, a man attains to oneness with Brahman.

THIRD CHAPTER
The Way of Action

Arjuna said:

1. If, O Janârdana, according to Thee, knowledge is superior to action, why then, O Keshava, dost Thou engage me in this terrible action?

2. With these seemingly conflicting words, Thou art, as it were, bewildering my understanding;—tell me that one thing for certain, by which I can attain to the highest.

The Blessed Lord said:

3. In the beginning (of creation), O sinless one, the twofold path of devotion was given by Me to this world;—the path of knowledge for the meditative, the path of work for the active.[68]

---

world of plurality alone and God is a nonentity to him.
It follows, that non-susceptibility to the influences of Nature, that is, perfect self-control (spoken of in the preceding sloka) is quite as natural a trait of the illumined soul as its opposite is of the ignorant.

66 The ocean is not at all affected by the waters flowing into it from all sides. Similarly, that man alone finds true peace in whom no reaction of desire is produced by the objects of enjoyment, which he happens to come across during his sojourn on earth.

67 The man who lives,—merely to work out his past Karma.

68 Meditative—those who prefer meditation to external action.
Active—those who believe in external work with or without meditation.

4. By non-performance of work none reaches worklessness; by merely giving up action no one attains to perfection.[69]

5. Verily none can ever rest for even an instant, without performing action; for all are made to act, helplessly indeed, by the Gunas, born of Prakriti.[70]

6. He, who restraining the organs of action, sits revolving in the mind, thoughts regarding objects of senses, he, of deluded understanding, is called a hypocrite.

7. But, who, controlling the senses by the mind, unattached, directs his organs of action to the path of work, he, O Arjuna, excels.

8. Do thou perform obligatory[71] action; for action is superior to inaction, and even the bare maintenance of thy body would not be possible if thou art inactive.

9. The world is bound by actions other than those performed for the sake of Yajna; do thou therefore, O son of Kunti, perform action for Yajna alone, devoid of attachment.[72]

10. The Prajâpati, having in the beginning created mankind together with Yajna, said,—"By this shall ye multiply: this shall be the milch cow of your desires.[73]

11. "Cherish the Devas with this, and may those Devas cherish you: thus cherishing one another, ye shall gain the highest good.[74]

12. "The Devas, cherished by Yajna, will give you desired-for objects." So, he who enjoys objects given by the Devas without offering (in return) to them, is verily a thief.

69 Worklessness and perfection: These are synonymous terms, meaning, becoming one with the Infinite and free from all ideas of want. A man who has reached this state can have no necessity or desire for work as a means to an end. Perfect satisfaction in the Self is his natural condition. (Vide III. 17.)

70 All are made to act: All men living under bondage.

71 See comment on V. 13.

72 Yajna: means a religious rite, sacrifice, worship: Or an action done with a good or spiritual motive. It also means the Deity. The Taittiriya-Samhitâ (I. 7. 4.) says, "Yajna is Vishnu Himself."

73 Prajâpati—the creator or Brahma.

74 Devas: (lit. the shining ones) beings much higher than man in the scale of evolution, who are in charge of cosmic functions.

13. The good, eating the remnants of Yajna, are freed from all sins: but who cook food (only) for themselves, those sinful ones eat sin.[75]

14. From food come forth beings: from rain food is produced: from Yajna arises rain and Yajna is born of Karma.[76]

15. Know Karma to have risen from the Veda, and the Veda from the Imperishable. Therefore the all-pervading Veda is ever centred in Yajna. [77]

16. He, who here follows not the wheel thus set revolving, living in sin, and satisfied in the senses, O son of Prithâ,—he lives in vain.[78]

17. But the man who is devoted to the Self, and is satisfied with the Self, and content in the Self alone, he has no obligatory duty.

18. He has no object in this world (to gain) by doing (an action), nor (does he incur any loss) by non-performance of action,—nor has he (need of) depending on any being for any object.

19. Therefore, do thou always perform actions which are obligatory, without attachment;—by performing action without attachment, one attains to the highest.

20. Verily by action alone, Janaka and others attained perfection;—

75 Deva-Yajna: offering sacrifices to the gods, Brahma-Yajna: teaching and reciting the Scriptures, Pitri-Yajna: offering libations of water to one's ancestors, Nri-Yajna: the feeding of the hungry, and Bhuta-Yajna: the feeding of the lower animals;—are the five daily duties enjoined on householders. The performance of these duties frees them from the fivefold sin, inevitable to a householder's life, due to the killing of life, from the use of, (1) the pestle and mortar, (2) the grinding-stone, (3) the oven, (4) the water-jar, and (5) the broom.

76 Yajna: Here it denotes not the sacrificial deeds themselves but the subtle principle, into which they are converted, after they have been performed, to appear, later on, as their fruits. This is technically known as Apurva.
Karma or sacrificial deeds prescribed in the Vedas.

77 All-pervading Veda: because it illumines all subjects and is the store of all knowledge, being the out-breathing of the Omniscient. It is said to be ever centred in Yajna, because it deals chiefly with Yajna, as the means of achieving the end, either of prosperity or final liberation, according as it is performed with or without desire.

78 The wheel of action started by Prajâpati on the basis of Veda and sacrifice.

also, simply with the view for the guidance of men, thou shouldst perform action.[79]

21. Whatsoever the superior person does, that is followed by others. What he demonstrates by action, that, people follow.

22. I have, O son of Prithâ, no duty, nothing that I have not gained, and nothing that I have to gain, in the three worlds; yet, I continue in action.

23. If ever I did not continue in work, without relaxation, men, O son of Prithâ, would in every way, follow in My wake.

24. If I did not do work, these worlds would perish. I should be the cause of the admixture of races, and I should ruin these beings.

25. As do the unwise, attached to work, act, so should the wise act, O descendant of Bharata, (but) without attachment, desirous of the guidance of the world.

26. One should not unsettle the understanding of the ignorant, attached to action; the wise, (himself) steadily acting, should engage (the ignorant) in all work.

27. The Gunas of Prakriti perform all action. With the understanding deluded by egoism, man thinks, "I am the doer."

28. But, one, with true insight into the domains of Guna and Karma, knowing that Gunas as senses merely rest on Gunas as objects, does not become attached.[80]

29. Men of perfect knowledge should not unsettle (the understanding of) people of dull wit and imperfect knowledge, who deluded by the Gunas of Prakriti attach (themselves) to the functions of the Gunas.[81]

30. Renouncing all actions to Me, with mind centred on the Self, getting rid of hope and selfishness, fight,—free from (mental) fever.

---

79 Guidance of men: the Sanskrit word means, gathering of men,—that is, into the right path.

80 With true insight etc.: Knowing the truth that the Self is distinct from all Gunas, and actions.

81 Those of imperfect knowledge—those who can only see as far as the immediate effect of actions.

31. Those men who constantly practise this teaching of Mine, full of Shraddhâ and without cavilling, they too, are freed from work.[82]

32. But those who decrying this teaching of Mine do not practise (it), deluded in all knowledge, and devoid of discrimination, know them to be ruined.

33. Even a wise man acts in accordance with his own nature: beings follow nature: what can restraint do?[83]

34. Attachment and aversion of the senses for their respective objects are natural: let none come under their sway: they are his foes.[84]

35. Better is one's own Dharma, (though) imperfect, than the Dharma of another well-performed. Better is death in one's own Dharma: the Dharma of another is fraught with fear.[85]

Arjuna said:

36. But by what impelled does man commit sin, though against his wishes, O Vârshneya, constrained as it were, by force?[86]

The Blessed Lord said:

37. It is desire—it is anger, born of the Rajo-guna: of great craving,

82 Shraddhâ: is a mental attitude constituted primarily of sincerity of purpose, humility, reverence and faith. You have Shraddhâ for your Guru—it is sincere reverence. You have Shraddhâ for the Gita —it is admiration for those of its teachings you understand and faith in those that you do not. You give alms to a beggar with Shraddhâ—it is a sense of humility combined with the hope that what you give will be acceptable and serviceable.

83 The reason why some people do not follow the teaching of the Lord is explained here: Their (lower) nature proves too strong for them.

84 His: of the seeker after truth.

Though, as has been said in the foregoing Sloka, some are so completely under the sway of their natural propensities, that restraint is of no avail to them, yet the seeker after truth should never think of following their example, but should always exert himself to overrule all attachment and aversion of the senses for their objects.

85 The implication is that Arjuna's thought of desisting from fight and going in for the calm and peaceful life of the Brahman is promoted by man's natural desire to shun what is disagreeable and embrace what is agreeable to the senses. He should on no account yield to this weakness.

86 Vârshneya: a descendant of the race of Vrishni.

and of great sin; know this as the foe here (in this world).[87]

38. As fire is enveloped by smoke, as a mirror by dust, as an embryo by the secundine, so is it covered by that.[88]

39. Knowledge is covered by this, the constant foe of the wise, O son of Kunti, the unappeasable fire of desire.[89]

40. The senses, the mind and the intellect are said to be its abode: through these, it deludes the embodied by veiling his wisdom.[90]

41. Therefore, O Bull of the Bharata race, controlling the senses at the outset, kill it,—the sinful, the destroyer of knowledge and realisation.

42. The senses are said to be superior (to the body); the mind is superior to the senses; the intellect is superior to the mind; and that which is superior to the intellect is He (the Atman).

43. Thus, knowing Him who is superior to the intellect, and restraining the self by the Self, destroy, O mighty-armed, that enemy, the unseizable foe, desire.

---

87 It is desire etc.: anger is only another form of desire,—desire obstructed. (See Note, II. 62-63).

88 "It" is knowledge, and "that" is desire, as explained in the following Sloka.

Three stages of the overclouding of knowledge or Self by desire are described by the three illustrations here given. The first stage is Sâttvika,—fire enveloped by smoke:—the rise of a slight wind of discrimination dispels the smoke of desire in a Sâttvika heart. The second, the Râjasika,—the dust on a mirror, requires some time and preparation. While the third,—the Tâmasika, takes a much longer time, like the release of the embryo from the afterbirth.

89 Desire is undoubtedly the foe of all mankind. Why it is said to be the constant foe of the wise, is that they feel it to be so even when under its sway. Fools are awakened for a moment only, when they suffer from its painful reactions.

90 Like a wise general, Krishna points out the fortress of the enemy, by conquering which the enemy is easily defeated.

Through these: by vitiating the senses, mind and the intellect.

FOURTH CHAPTER
The Way of Renunciation of Action in Knowledge.

The Blessed Lord said:

1. I told this imperishable Yoga to Vivasvat; Vivasvat told it to Manu; (and) Manu told it to Ikshvâku:[91]

2. Thus handed down in regular succession, the royal sages knew it. This Yoga, by long lapse of time, declined in this world, O burner of foes.

3. I have this day told thee that same ancient Yoga, (for) thou art My devotee, and My friend, and this secret is profound indeed.[92]

Arjuna said:

4. Later was Thy birth, and that of Vivasvat prior; how then should I understand that Thou toldest this in the beginning?

The Blessed Lord said:

5. Many are the births that have been passed by Me and thee, O Arjuna. I know them all, whilst thou knowest not, O scorcher of foes.

6. Though I am unborn, of changeless nature and Lord of beings, yet subjugating My Prakriti, I come into being by My own Mâyâ.[93]

7. Whenever, O descendant of Bharata, there is decline of Dharma, and rise of Adharma, then I body Myself forth.[94]

---

91 Vivasvat: the Sun. Manu: the law-giver. Ikshvâku was the famous ancestor of the Solar dynasty of Kshatriyas.
This Yoga is said to be imperishable, because the end attainable through it is imperishable.

92 Secret: Not as the privilege of an individual or a sect, but because of its profundity. It is a secret to the unworthy only.

93 Subjugating My Prakriti: He does not come into being as others do, bound by Karma, under the thraldom of Prakriti (Nature). He is not tied by the fetters of the Gunas—because He is the Lord of Mâyâ.
By My own Mâyâ: My embodiment is only apparent grid does not touch My true nature.

94 The Dharma and its opposite Adharma imply all the duties (and their

8. For the protection of the good, for the destruction of the wicked, and for the establishment of Dharma, I come into being in every age.[95]

9. He who thus knows, in true light, My divine birth and action, leaving the body, is not born again: he attains to Me, O Arjuna.[96]

10. Freed from attachment, fear and anger, absorbed in Me, taking refuge in Me, purified by the fire of Knowledge, many have attained My Being.[97]

11. In whatever way men worship Me, in the same way do I fulfil their desires: (it is) My path, O son of Prithâ, (that) men tread, in all ways. [98]

12. Longing for success in action, in this world, (men) worship the gods. Because success, resulting from action, is, quickly attained in the human world.[99]

13. The fourfold caste was created by Me, by the differentiation of Guna and Karma. Though I am the author thereof, know Me to be the non-doer, and changeless.[100]

---

opposites) as ordained for men in different stations by the definite scheme of their life and salvation.

95 Destruction of the wicked: in order to destroy their wickedness, and give them life eternal.

96 He who knows &c.: He who knows the great truth,—that the Lord though apparently born is ever beyond birth and death, though apparently active in the cause of righteousness, is ever beyond all action,—becomes illumined with Self-knowledge. Such a man is never born again.

97 Many have attained: The import is that the path of liberation here taught by Sri Krishna is not of recent origin, nor is it dependent upon His present manifestation, but has been handed down from time immemorial.

98 In this sloka Sri Krishna anticipates the objection that God is partial to some and unkind to others, since He blesses some with Self-knowledge and leaves the rest in darkness and misery. This difference is not due to any difference in His attitude towards them, but is of their own choice.
My path: In the whole region of thought and action, wherever there is fulfilment of object, no matter what, the same is due to the Lord. As the Self within, He brings to fruition all wishes, when the necessary conditions are fulfilled.

99 Because success . . . human world: Worldly success is much easier of attainment than Self-knowledge. Hence it is that the ignorant do not go in for the latter.

100 This sloka is intended to explain the diversity of human temperaments and tendencies. All men are not of the same nature, because of the preponderance

14. Actions do not taint Me, nor have I any thirst for the result of action. He who knows Me thus is not fettered by action.[101]

15. Knowing thus, the ancient seekers after freedom also performed action. Do thou, therefore, perform action, as did the ancients in olden times.[102]

16. Even sages are bewildered, as to what is action and what is inaction. I shall therefore tell you what action is, by knowing which you will be freed from evil.[103]

17. For verily, (the true nature) even of action (enjoined by the Shâstras) should be known, as also, (that) of forbidden action, and of inaction: the nature of Karma is impenetrable.

18. He who sees inaction in action, and action in inaction, he is intelligent among men, he is a Yogi and a doer of all action.[104]

19. Whose undertakings are all devoid of plan and desire for results, and whose actions are burnt by the fire of knowledge, him, the sages call

---

of the different Gunas in them.

The caste system was originally meant to make perfect the growth of humanity, by the special culture of certain features, through the process of discriminate selection.

Though I am the author &c.: The Lord, though the author of the caste system, is yet not the author. The same dread of being taken as a doer or an agent crops up again and again. The paradox is explained in Chap. IX. 5-10. Mâyâ is the real author. He is taken as such, because it is His light which gives existence, not only to all actions, but to Mâyâ herself.

101 Actions do not taint Me: Karma cannot introduce into Me anything foreign. I never depart from My true Self, which is All-fullness.

102 Knowing thus: Taking this point of view, that is, that the Self can have no desire for the fruits of action and cannot be soiled by action.

103 Evil: the evil of existence, the wheel of birth and death.

104 An action is an action so long as the idea of actor-ness of the Self holds good. Directly the idea of actor-ness disappears, no matter what or how much is done, action has lost its nature. It has become harmless: it can no longer bind. On the other hand, how much soever inactive an ignorant person may remain, so long as there is the idea of actor-ness in him, he is constantly doing action. Action equals to belief in the actor-ness of oneself and inaction its reverse.

He is the doer of all action: He has achieved the end of all action, which is freedom.

wise.[105]

20. Forsaking the clinging to fruits of action, ever satisfied, depending on nothing, though engaged in action, he does not do anything.

21. Without hope, the body and mind controlled and all possessions relinquished, he does not suffer any evil consequences, by doing mere bodily action.[106]

22. Content with what comes to him without effort, unaffected by the pairs of opposites, free from envy, even-minded in success and failure, though acting, he is not bound.

23. Devoid of attachment, liberated, with mind centred in knowledge, performing work for Yajna alone, his whole Karma dissolves away.

24. The process is Brahman, the clarified butter is Brahman, offered by Brahman in the fire of Brahman; by seeing Brahman in action, he reaches Brahman alone.[107]

25. Some Yogis perform sacrifices to Devas alone, while others offer the self as sacrifice by the self in the fire of Brahman alone.[108]

26. Some again offer hearing and other senses as sacrifice in the fire of control, while others offer sound and other sense-objects as sacrifice in the fire of the senses.[109]

27. Some again offer all the actions of the senses and the functions of the vital energy, as sacrifice in the fire of control in self, kindled by knowledge.

---

105 Whose undertakings &c.: Who is devoid of egoism.

106 Evil consequences: resulting from good and bad actions, for both lead to bondage.

107 How can the whole Karma of a person engaged in work melt away as stated here? Because after knowledge, his whole life becomes one act of Yajna, in which the process of oblation, the offering, the fire, the doer of the sacrifice, the work, and the goal, are all Brahman. Since his Karma produces no other result than the attainment of Brahman, his Karma is said to melt away.

108 Others offer &c.: The sacrifice referred to here, is, divesting the Self of Its Upâdhis (limiting adjuncts), so that It is found to be the Self.

109 Others offer sound &c.: Others direct their senses towards pure and unforbidden objects, and in so doing regard themselves as performing acts of sacrifice.

28. Others again offer wealth, austerity, and Yoga, as sacrifice, while still others, of self-restraint and rigid vows, offer study of the scriptures and knowledge, as sacrifice.[110]

29. Yet some offer as sacrifice, the outgoing into the in-coming breath, and the in-coming into the out-going, stopping the courses of the in-coming and out-going breaths, constantly practising the regulation of the vital energy; while others yet of regulated food, offer in the Prânas the functions thereof.[111]

30-31. All of these are knowers of Yajna, having their sins consumed by Yajna, and eating of the nectar—the remnant of Yajna, they go to the Eternal Brahman. (Even) this world is not for the non-performer of Yajna, how then another, O best of the Kurus?[112]

32. Various Yajnas, like the above, are strewn in the store-house of the Veda. Know them all to be born of action, and thus knowing, thou shalt be free.[113]

33. Knowledge-sacrifice, O scorcher of foes, is superior to sacrifice (performed) with (material) objects. All action in its entirety, O Pârtha, attains its consummation in knowledge.

34. Know that, by prostrating thyself, by questions, and by service; the wise, those who have realised the Truth, will instruct thee in that

---

110 Offer Yoga as sacrifice: Practise the eightfold Yoga as an act of sacrifice.

111 Offer in the Prânas the functions thereof: Whatever Prâna has been controlled, into it they sacrifice all other Prânas; these latter become, as it were, merged in the former. Or, in another way: They control the different Prânas and unify them by the foregoing method; the senses are thus attenuated and are merged in the unified Prâna, as an act of sacrifice.

All the various acts described in verses 25 to 29, as offerings of sacrifice, are only conceived as such, the study of the scriptures is regarded as an act of sacrifice, and so on.

112 They go to the Eternal Brahman: in course of time, after attaining knowledge through purification of heart.

Even this world is not for the non-performer of Yajna: this means,—he that does not perform any of the Yajnas above mentioned, is not fit even for this wretched human world,—how then could he hope to gain a better world than this?

113 Strewn in the store-house of the Veda: inculcated by or known through the Veda.

knowledge.[114]

35. Knowing which, thou shalt not, O Pândava, again get deluded like this, and by which thou shalt see the whole of creation in (thy) Self and in Me.[115]

36. Even if thou be the most sinful among all the sinful, yet by the raft of knowledge alone thou shalt go across all sin.

37. As blazing fire reduces wood into ashes, so, O Arjuna, does the fire of knowledge reduce all Karma to ashes.[116]

38. Verily there exists nothing in this world purifying like knowledge. In good time, having reached perfection in Yoga, one realises that oneself in one's own heart.

39. The man with Shraddhâ, the devoted, the master of one's senses, attains (this) knowledge. Having attained knowledge one goes at once to the Supreme Peace.

40. The ignorant, the man without Shraddhâ, the doubting self, goes to destruction. The doubting self has neither this world, nor the next, nor happiness.[117]

41. With work renounced by Yoga and doubts rent asunder by knowledge, O Dhananjaya, actions do not bind him who is poised in the Self.

---

114 Prostration before the Guru, questions and personal services to him, constitute discipleship.

Those who have realised the Truth: mere theoretical knowledge, however perfect, does not qualify a person to be a Guru: the Truth, or Brahman, must be realised, before one can claim that most elevated position.

115 Which: the knowledge referred to in the preceding sloka to be learnt from the Guru.

116 Excepting of course the Prârabdha, or Karma which, causing the present body, has begun to bear fruits.

117 The ignorant: one who knows not the Self.

The man without Shraddhâ: one who has no faith in the words and teachings of his Guru.

The doubting self has &c.: One of a doubting disposition fails to enjoy this world, owing to his constantly rising suspicion about the people, and things around him, and is also full of doubt as regards the next world; so do the ignorant and the man without Shraddhâ.

42. Therefore, cutting with the sword of knowledge, this doubt about the Self, born of ignorance, residing in thy heart, take refuge in Yoga. Arise, O Bhârata!

FIFTH CHAPTER
The Way of Renunciation

Arjuna said:

1. Renunciation of action, O Krishna, thou commendest, and again, its performance. Which is the better one of these? Do thou tell me decisively.[118]

The Blessed Lord said:

2. Both renunciation and performance of action lead to freedom: of these, performance of action is superior to the renunciation of action.[119]

3. He should be known a constant Sannyâsi, who neither likes nor dislikes: for, free from the pairs of opposites, mighty-armed, he is easily set free from bondage.[120]

4. Children, not the wise, speak of knowledge and performance of action, as distinct. He who truly lives in one, gains the fruits of both.[121]

---

118 In IV. 18, 19, 21, 22, 24, 32, 33, 37 and 41, the Lord has spoken of the renunciation of all actions; and in IV. 42 He has exhorted Arjuna to engage in Yoga, in performance of action. Owing to the mutual opposition between the two, which makes it impossible for one man to resort to both of them at the same time, doubt arises in the mind of Arjuna, and hence the question as above.
Its performance—"Yoga" in the test: Yoga here and in the following verses means Karma-Yoga.
119 Performance of action—is superior to mere renunciation (i.e., unaccompanied with knowledge) in the case of the novice in the path of spirituality. See the 6th sloka of this chapter.
120 Constant Sannyâsi: he need not have taken Sannyâsa formally, but if he has the above frame of mind, he is a Sannyâsi for ever and aye.
Neither likes nor dislikes: Neither hates pain and the objects causing pain, nor desires pleasure and the objects causing pleasure, though engaged in action.
121 Children: the ignorant people devoid of insight into the purpose of the Shâstra.

5. The plane which is reached by the Jnânins is also reached by the Karmayogins. Who sees knowledge and performance of action as one, he sees.

6. Renunciation of action, O mighty-armed, is hard to attain to without performance of action; the man of meditation, purified by devotion to action, quickly goes to Brahman.[122]

7. With the mind purified by devotion to performance of action, and the body conquered, and senses subdued, one who realises one's Self, as the Self in all beings, though acting, is not tainted.

8-9. The knower of Truth, (being) centred (in the Self) should think, "I do nothing at all"—though seeing, hearing, touching, smelling, eating, going, sleeping, breathing, speaking, letting go, holding, opening and closing the eyes—convinced that it is the senses that move among sense-objects.

10. He who does actions forsaking attachment, resigning them to Brahman, is not soiled by evil, like unto a lotus-leaf by water.[123]

11. Devotees in the path of work perform action, only with body, mind, senses, and intellect, forsaking attachment, for the purification of the heart.[124]

12. The well-poised, forsaking the fruit of action, attains peace, born of steadfastness; the unbalanced one, led by desire, is bound by being attached to the fruit (of action).[125]

13. The subduer (of the senses), having renounced all actions by discrimination, rests happily in the city of the nine gates, neither acting,

---

122 It is not that renunciation of action based on knowledge is not superior to performance of action, but that the latter method is easier for a beginner, and qualifies him for the higher path, by purifying his mind. Hence it is the proper, and therefore the superior course, in his case.

123 Evil: the results, good and bad, producing bondage.

124 Only with &c.—without egotism or selfishness: it applies to body, mind, senses and intellect.

125 Born of steadfastness: Sankara explains Naisthikim as gradual perfection in the path of knowledge, having the following stages of development: (1) purity of heart, (2) gaining of knowledge, (3) renunciation of action, (4) steadiness in knowledge.

nor causing (others) to act.[126]

14. Neither agency, nor actions does the Lord create for the world, nor (does He bring about) the union with the fruit of action. It is universal ignorance that does. (it all).

15. The Omnipresent takes note of the merit or demerit of none. Knowledge is enveloped in ignorance, hence do beings get deluded.[127]

16. But whose ignorance is destroyed by the knowledge of Self,—that knowledge of theirs, like the sun, reveals the Supreme (Brahman).

17. Those who have their intellect absorbed in That, whose self is That, whose steadfastness is in That, whose consummation is That, their impurities cleansed by knowledge, they attain to Non-return (Moksha).

18. The knowers of the Self look with an equal eye on a Brâhmana endowed with learning and humility, a cow, an elephant, a dog, and a pariah.[128]

19. (Relative) existence has been conquered by them, even in this world, whose mind rests in evenness, since Brahman is even and without imperfection: therefore they indeed rest in Brahman.[129]

126 All actions: 1st, Nitya, or obligatory—the performance of which does not produce any merit while the non-performance produces demerit. 2nd, Naimittika, those arising on the occurrence of some special events, as the birth of a son: these also are customary. 3rd, Kâmya—those intended for securing some special ends: these are only optional. 4th, Nishiddha—or forbidden. He rests happily in the body (of nine organic openings), seeing inaction in action: just exhausting his Prârabdha—not relating or identifying himself with anything of the dual universe.

127 In unmistakable words, Krishna describes the position of Iswara, or the Lord, in relation to the Universe, in these two verses.

He is all-blissful, all-perfect; even the shadow of a motive or relation in Him, would be contradictory to His nature. His mere proximity to Prakriti or Nature endues the latter with power and potency of causing all that is. Jiva is bound so long as it, relates itself to, and identifies itself with this Nature. When it ceases to do so, it attains freedom. The whole teaching of the Gita, and therefore of the whole Hindu Scripture, on this subject, is condensed in the above.

128 Because they can see nothing but the Self. It makes no difference to the sun whether it be reflected in the Ganges, in wine, in a small pool, or in any unclean liquid: the same is the case with the Self. No Upâdhi (or limiting adjunct) can attach to it.

129 Relative existence: All bondage as of birth, death etc. All possibility

20. Resting in Brahman, with intellect steady, and without delusion, the knower of Brahman neither rejoiceth on receiving what is pleasant, nor grieveth on receiving what is unpleasant.

21. With the heart unattached to external objects, he realises the joy that is in the Self. With the heart devoted to the meditation of Brahman, he attains un-decaying happiness.[130]

22. Since enjoyments that are contact-born are parents of misery alone, and with beginning and end, O son of Kunti, a wise man does not seek pleasure in them.

23. He who can withstand in this world, before the liberation from the body, the impulse arising from lust and anger, he is steadfast (in Yoga), he is a happy man.

24. Whose happiness is within, whose relaxation is within, whose light is within, that Yogi alone, becoming Brahman, gains absolute freedom. [131]

25. With imperfections exhausted, doubts dispelled, senses controlled, engaged in the good of all beings, the Rishis obtain absolute freedom.[132]

26. Released from lust and anger, the heart controlled, the Self realised, absolute freedom is for such Sannyâsis, both here and hereafter.

27-28. Shutting out external objects, steadying the eyes between the eyebrows, restricting the even currents of Prâna and Apâna inside the nostrils; the senses, mind, and intellect controlled, with Moksha as the supreme goal, freed from desire, fear and anger: such a man of meditation is verily free for ever.[133]

---

of bondage is destroyed when the mind attains perfect evenness, which in other words means—becoming Brahman.

130 Heart—Antah-karana.

131 Within: In the Self.

Absolute Freedom: Brahma-Nirvâna. He attains Moksha while still living in the body.

132 Rishis: Men of right vision and renunciation.

133 External objects: Sound and other sense-objects. External objects are shut out from the mind by not thinking of them. When the eyes are half-closed in meditation, the eye-balls remain fixed, and their gaze converges, as it were, between the eyebrows. Prâna is the out-going breath, Apâna the in-coming; the restriction described is effected by Prânâyâma.

These two verses are the aphorisms of which the following chapter is the

29. Knowing Me as the dispenser of Yajnas and asceticisms, as the Great Lord of all worlds, as the friend of all beings, he attains Peace.[134]

SIXTH CHAPTER
The Way of Meditation

The Blessed Lord said:

1. He who performs his bounden duty without leaning to the fruit of action —he is a renouncer of action as well as of steadfast mind: not he who is without fire, nor he who is without action.[135]

2. Know that to be devotion to action, which is called renunciation, O Pândava, for none becomes a devotee to action without forsaking Sankalpa.[136]

3. For the man of meditation wishing to attain purification of heart leading to concentration, work is said to be the way: For him, when he has attained such (concentration), inaction is said to be the way.[137]

4. Verily, when there is no attachment, either to sense-objects, or to actions, having renounced all Sankalpas, then is one said to have attained

---

commentary.

134 Dispenser: Both as author and goal, the Lord is the dispenser of the fruit of all actions.

Friend: Doer of good without expecting any return.

135 Bounden duty: Nityakarma.

Renouncer of action as well as of steadfast mind: Sannyâsi and Yogi.

Without fire: He that has renounced actions enjoined by the Vedas, requiring fire as adjunct, e.g., Agnihotra.

Without action: He who has renounced actions which do not require fire as adjunct, such as austerities and meritorious acts like digging wells etc.

136 Sankalpa—is the working of the imaging faculty, forming fancies, making plans and again brushing them aside, conceiving future results, starting afresh on a new line, leading to different issues, and so on and so forth. No one can be a Karma-Yogin or a devotee to action, who makes plans and wishes for the fruit of action.

137 Purification of the heart leading to concentration—Yoga. "For a Brâhmana there is no wealth like unto (the eye of) one-ness, (and) evenness, trueness, refinement, steadiness, harmlessness, straightforwardness, and gradual withdrawal from all action."—Mahâbhârata, Shânti Parva. 175, 88.

concentration.[138]

5. A man should uplift himself by his own self, so let him not weaken this self. For this self is the friend of oneself, and this self is the enemy of oneself.[139]

6. The self (the active part of our nature) is the friend of the self, for him who has conquered himself by this self. But to the unconquered self, this self is inimical, (and behaves) like (an external) foe.[140]

7. To the self-controlled and serene, the Supreme Self is, the object of constant, realisation, in cold and heat, pleasure and pain, as well as in honour and dishonour.[141]

8. Whose heart is filled with satisfaction by wisdom and realisation, and is changeless, whose senses are conquered, and to whom a lump of earth, stone, and gold are the same: that Yogi is called steadfast.[142]

9. He attains excellence who looks with equal regard upon well-wishers, friends, foes, neutrals, arbiters, the hateful, the relatives, and upon the righteous and the unrighteous alike.

10. The Yogi should constantly practise concentration of the heart, retiring into solitude, alone, with the mind and body subdued, and free from hope and possession.

---

138 Attained concentration: Yogârudha.
Renouncer of all Sankalpas: "O desire, I know where thy root lies: thou art born of Sankalpa. I shall not think of thee, and thou shalt cease to exist, together with thy root." Mahâbhârata. Shânti Parva. 177, 25.

139 The self-conscious nature of man is here considered in two aspects as being both the object of spiritual uplift and the subject of spiritual uplift, the ego acted upon and the ego acting upon the former. This latter active principle or ego should be kept strong in its uplifting function, for it. is apt to turn an enemy, if it is not a friend, and the next verse explains the reason.

140 The self is the friend of one, in whom the aggregate of the body and the senses has been brought under control, and an enemy when such in not the case.

141 Hence he remains unruffled in pleasant and adverse environments.

142 Wisdom—Jnâna: knowledge of Shâstras. Realisation—Vijnâna: one's own experience of the teachings of Shâstras.
Changeless—like the anvil. Things are hammered and shaped on the anvil, but the anvil remains unchanged: in the same manner he is called Kutastha—whose heart remains unchanged though objects are present.

11. Having in a cleanly spot established his seat, firm, neither too high nor too low, made of a cloth, a skin, and Kusha-grass, arranged in consecution:[143]

12. There, seated on that seat, making the mind one-pointed and subduing the action of the imaging faculty and the senses, let him practise Yoga for the purification of the heart.

13. Let him firmly hold his body, head and neck erect and still, (with the eye-balls fixed, as if) gazing at the tip of his nose, and not looking around.[144]

14. With the heart serene and fearless, firm in the vow of a Brahmachâri, with the mind controlled, and ever thinking of Me, let him sit (in Yoga) having Me as his supreme goal.

15. Thus always keeping the mind steadfast, the Yogi of subdued mind attains the peace residing in Me,—the peace which culminates in Nirvâna (Moksha).

16. (Success in) Yoga is not for him who eats too much or too little—nor, O Arjuna, for him who sleeps too much or too little.[145]

17. To him who is temperate in eating and recreation, in his effort for work, and in sleep and wakefulness, Yoga becomes the destroyer of misery.

18. When the completely controlled mind rests serenely in the Self alone, free from longing after all desires, then is one called steadfast, (in the Self).

19. "As a lamp in a spot sheltered from the wind does not flicker,"—even such has been the simile used for a Yogi of subdued mind, practising concentration in the Self.

20-23. When the mind, absolutely restrained by the practice of

143 Arranged in consecution: that is,—the Kusha-grass arranged on the ground; above that, a tiger or deer skin, covered by a cloth.

144 Gazing at the tip of his nose,—could not be-literally meant here, because then the mind would be fixed only there, and not on the Self: when the eyes are half-closed in meditation, and the eye-balls are still, the gaze is directed, as it were, on the tip of the nose.

145 The Yoga-shâstra prescribes: "Half (the stomach) for food and condiments, the third (quarter) for water, and the fourth should be reserved for free motion of air."

concentration, attains quietude, and when seeing the Self by the self, one is satisfied in his own Self; when he feels that infinite bliss—which is perceived by the (purified) intellect and which transcends the senses, and established wherein he never departs from his real state; and having obtained which, regards no other acquisition superior to that, and where established, he is not moved even by heavy sorrow;—let that be known as the state, called by the name of Yoga,—a state of severance from the contact of pain. This Yoga should be practised with perseverance, undisturbed by depression of heart.[146]

24. Abandoning without reserve all desires born of Sankalpa, and completely restraining, by the mind alone, the whole group of senses from their objects in all directions;

25. With the intellect set in patience, with the mind fastened on the Self, let him attain quietude by degrees: let him not think of anything.

26. Through whatever reason the restless, unsteady mind wanders away, let him curbing it from that, bring it under the subjugation of the Self alone.

27. Verily, the supreme bliss comes to that Yogi, of perfectly tranquil mind, with passions quieted, Brahman-become, and freed from taint.[147]

28. The Yogi freed from taint (of good and evil), constantly engaging the mind thus, with ease attains the infinite bliss of contact with Brahman.

29. With the heart concentrated by Yoga, with the eye of evenness for all things, he beholds the Self in all beings and all beings in the Self.

30. He who sees Me in all things, and sees all things in Me, he never becomes separated from Me, nor do I become separated from him.[148]

31. He who being established in unity, worships Me, who am dwelling

---

146 Which is perceived . . . intellect: Which the purified intellect can grasp independently of the senses. When in meditation the mind is deeply concentrated, the senses do not function and are resolved into their cause,—that is, the mind; and when the latter is steady, so that there is only the intellect functioning, or in other words, cognition only exists, the indescribable Self is realised.

147 Brahman-become, i.e., one who has realised that all is Brahman. Taint—of good and evil.

148 Separated, i.e., by time, space, or anything intervening.

in all beings, whatever his mode of life, that Yogi abides in Me.[149]

32. He who judges of pleasure or pain everywhere, by the same standard as he applies to himself, that Yogi, O Arjuna, is regarded as the highest.[150]

Arjuna said:

33. This Yoga which has been taught by Thee, O slayer of Madhu, as characterised by evenness, I do not see (the possibility of) its lasting endurance, owing to restlessness (of the mind).

34. Verily, the mind, O Krishna, is restless, turbulent, strong, and unyielding;. I regard it quite as hard to achieve its control, as that of the wind.[151]

The Blessed Lord said:

35. Without doubt, O mighty-armed, the mind is restless, and difficult to control; but through practice and renunciation, O son of Kunti, it may be governed.[152]

36. Yoga is hard to be attained by one of uncontrolled self: such is My conviction; but the self-controlled, striving by right means, can obtain it.

Arjuna said:

37. Though possessed of Shraddhâ but unable to control himself, with the mind wandering away from Yoga, what end does one, failing to gain perfection in Yoga, meet, O Krishna?

---

149 Worships Me: realises Me as the Self of all.
Established in unity, i.e., having resolved all duality in the underlying unity.

150 Seeing that whatever is pleasure or pain to, himself, is alike pleasure or pain to all beings, he, the highest of Yogins, wishes good to all and evil to none,—he is always harmless and compassionate to all creatures.

151 'Krishna,' is derived from 'Krish,' to scrape: Krishna is so called, because He scrapes or draws away all sins and other evils from His devotees.

152 Cf. Patanjali I. 12.
Practice: Earnest and repeated attempt to make the mind steady in its unmodified state of Pure Intelligence, by means of constant meditation upon the chosen Ideal.
Renunciation: Freedom from desire for any pleasures, seen or unseen, achieved by a constant perception of evil in them.

38. Does he not, fallen from both, perish, without support, like a rent cloud, O mighty-armed, deluded in the path of Brahman?[153]

39. This doubt of mine, O Krishna, Thou shouldst completely dispel; for it is not possible for any but Thee to dispel this doubt.[154]

The Blessed Lord said:

40. Verily, O son of Prithâ, there is destruction for him, neither here nor hereafter: for, the doer of good, O my son, never comes to grief.[155]

41. Having attained to the worlds of the righteous, and dwelling there for everlasting years, one fallen from Yoga reincarnates in the home of the pure and the prosperous.[156]

42. Or else he is born into a family of wise Yogis only; verily, a birth such as that is very rare to obtain in this world.[157]

43. There he is united with the intelligence acquired in his former body, and strives more than before, for perfection, O son of the Kurus.[158]

44. By that previous practice alone, he is borne on in spite of himself. Even the enquirer after Yoga rises superior to the performer of Vedic actions.[159]

45. The Yogi, striving assiduously, purified of taint, gradually gaining

153 Fallen from both: That is, from both the paths of knowledge and action.

154 Since there can be no better teacher than the Omniscient Lord.

155 Tâta—son. A disciple is looked upon as a son; Arjuna is thus addressed having placed himself in the position of a disciple to Krishna.

156 Everlasting years—not absolutely, meaning a very long period.

157 Very rare: more difficult than the one mentioned in the preceding Sloka.

158 Intelligence—Samskâra: Store of experience in the shape of impressions and habits.

Strives . . . perfection: Strives more strenuously to attain to higher planes of realisation than those acquired in his former birth.

159 Borne on in spite of himself: carried to the goal of the course which he marked out for himself in his last incarnation, by the force of his former Samskâras, though he might be unconscious of them—or even unwilling to pursue it, owing to the interference of some untoward Karma.

Rises &c.: lit. goes beyond the Word-Brahman, i.e., the Vedas.

perfection through many births, then reaches the highest goal.

46. The Yogi is regarded as superior to those who practise asceticism, also to those who have obtained wisdom (through the Shâstras). He is also superior to the performers of action, (enjoined in the Vedas). Therefore, be thou a Yogi, O Arjuna![160]

47. And of all Yogis, he who with the inner self merged in Me, with Shraddhâ devotes himself to Me, is considered by Me the most steadfast.[161]

SEVENTH CHAPTER
The Way of Knowledge with Realisation

The Blessed Lord said:

1. With the mind intent on Me, O son of Prithâ, taking refuge in Me, and practising Yoga, how thou shalt without doubt know Me fully, that do thou hear.[162]

2. I shall tell you in full, of knowledge, speculative and practical, knowing which, nothing more here remains to be known.

3. One, perchance, in thousands of men, strives for perfection; and one perchance, among the blessed ones, striving thus, knows Me in reality.[163]

4. Bhumi (earth), Ap (water), Anala (fire), Vâyu (air), Kha (ether), mind, intellect, and egoism: thus is My Prakriti divided eight-fold.[164]

160 Wisdom: Knowledge from precepts, but not direct insight into the Divine Truth.

161 Of all Yogis &c.:—of all Yogis he who devotes himself to the All-pervading Infinite, is superior to those who devote themselves to the lesser ideals, or gods, such as Vasu, Rudra, Aditya, etc.

162 Fully, i.e., possessed of infinite greatness, strength, power, grace, and other infinite attributes.

163 The Blessed: Siddhânâm—this word literally means the perfected ones—but here it means only those who having acquired good Karma in a past incarnation, strive for freedom in this life.

164 The raison d'être of this reduction of matter into five elements is quite different from that conceived by modern science. Man has five senses only,

5. This is the lower (Prakriti). But different from it, know thou, O mighty-armed, My higher Prakriti—the principle of self-consciousness, by which this universe is sustained.

6. Know that these (two Prakritis) are the womb of all beings. I am the origin and dissolution of the whole universe.[165]

7. Beyond Me, O Dhananjaya, there is naught. All this is strung in Me, as a row of jewels on a thread.[166]

8. I am the sapidity in waters, O son of Kunti; I, the radiance in the moon and the sun; I am the Om in all the Vedas, sound in Akâsha, and manhood in men.[167]

9. I am the sweet fragrance in earth, and the brilliance in fire am I; the life in all beings, and the austerity am I in ascetics.

10. Know Me, O son of Prithâ, as the eternal seed of all beings. I am the intellect of the intelligent, and the heroism of the heroic.

11. Of the strong, I am the strength devoid of desire and attachment. I am, O bull among the Bhâratas, desire in beings, unopposed to Dharma. [168]

---

just five ways in which he can be affected by matter, therefore his perception of matter cannot be divided further. The five elements are of two kinds, subtle and gross. The gross state is said 'to be formed by taking half of a subtle element, and adding ⅛th to it, of each of the rest: e.g., gross Akâsha = ½ subtle Akâsha + ⅛th subtle Vâyu + ⅛th subtle Tejas + ⅛th subtle Ap + ⅛th subtle Bhumi: Then again, the ether, air, light, water, and earth of modern science, do not answer to the five elements of Hindu philosophy. Akâsha is just the sound-producing agency. From Akâsha rises Vâyu, having the properties of sound and touch. From Vâyu springs Tejas, possessing the property of visibility, as well as those of its predecessors. From Tejas rises Ap, combining with the above properties its distinctive feature,—flavour. Bhumi comes from Ap, bringing the additional property of smell to its inheritance.

165 I am the origin &c.: In Me the whole universe originates and dissolves, as everything springs froth My Prakriti.

166 Beyond Me—there is no other cause of the universe but Me.

167 In Me as essence, all these are woven, as being My manifestations.

168 Desire—Kâma: thirst for objects not present to the senses.
Attachment—Râga: for those presented to the senses .
Unopposed to Dharma: the desire which moves in harmony with the ordained duties of life.

12. And whatever states pertaining to Sattva, and those pertaining to Rajas, and to Tamas, know them to proceed from Me alone; still I am not in them, but they are in Me.[169]

13. Deluded by these states, the modifications of the three Gunas (of Prakriti), all this world does not know Me, beyond them, and immutable.

14. Verily, this divine illusion of Mine, constituted of the Gunas, is difficult to cross over; those who devote themselves to Me alone, cross over this illusion.[170]

15. They do not devote themselves to Me,—the evil-doers, the deluded, the lowest of men, deprived of discrimination by Mâyâ, and following the way of the Asuras.[171]

16. Four kinds of virtuous men worship Me, O Arjuna,—the distressed, the seeker of knowledge, the seeker of enjoyment, and the wise, O bull among the Bhâratas.[172]

17. Of them, the wise man, ever-steadfast, (and fired) with devotion to the One, excels; for supremely dear am I to the wise, and he is dear to Me.

18. Noble indeed are they all, but the wise man I regard as My very Self; for with the mind steadfast, he is established in Me alone, as the supreme goal.

19. At the end of many births, the man of wisdom takes refuge in Me, realising that all this is Vâsudeva (the innermost Self). Very rare is that great soul.

---

169 All things are in Him, yet not He in them. Logically, this can' only happen in superimposition through illusion: as that of a ghost seen in the stump of a tree; the ghost is in the stump, from the point of view of the man in the dark, but the stump is never in the ghost. Similarly the universe is superimposed on the Lord, seen in His place through Mâyâ, but He is not in it. The Lord returns to the same teaching in Chap. IX. 4, 5.

170 Divine: transcending human perception.

Devote . . . alone: Abandoning all formal religion (Dharma) completely take refuge in Me, their own Self, the Lord of illusion.

171 Way of the Asuras, i.e., cruelty, untruth, and the like.

172 Seeker of enjoyment: One who wishes for objects of enjoyment, both here and hereafter.

The Wise: One who has forsaken all desires, knowing them to arise from Mâyâ.

20. Others again, deprived of discrimination by this or that desire, following this or that rite, devote themselves to other gods, led by their own natures.[173]

21. Whatsoever form any devotee seeks to worship with Shraddhâ,—that Shraddhâ of his do I make unwavering.

22. Endued with that Shraddhâ, he engages in the worship of that, and from it, gains his desires,—these being verily dispensed by Me alone.

23. But the fruit (accruing) to these men of little understanding is limited. The worshippers of the Devas go to the Devas; My devotees too come to me.[174]

24. The foolish regard Me, the un-manifested, as come into manifestation, not knowing My supreme state,—immutable and transcendental. [175]

25. Veiled by the illusion born of the congress of the Gunas, I am not manifest to all. This deluded world knows Me not, the Unborn, the Immutable.[176]

26. I know, O Arjuna, the beings of the whole past, and the present, and the future, but Me none knoweth.

27. By the delusion of the pairs of opposites, arising from desire and aversion, O descendant of Bharata, all beings fall into delusion at birth, O scorcher of foes.[177]

173 Own natures: Samskâras acquired in previous lives.

174 These men of little understanding: Though the amount of exertion is the same (in the two kinds of worship), these people do not take refuge in Me, by doing which they may attain infinite results.

175 The ignorant take Me as an ordinary mortal, assuming embodiment from the unmanifested state, like all other men, being impelled by the force of past Karma. This is due to their ignorance of My real nature; hence they do not worship Me, the One without a second.

176 This Yoga-Mâyâ spread over the Lord, which veils the understanding of others in recognising Him, does not obscure His own knowledge, as it is His, and He is the wielder of it,—just as the glamour (Mâyâ) caused by a juggler (Mâyâvin) does not obstruct his own knowledge. This illusion which binds others, cannot dim His vision.

177 To one whose mind is subject to the dualistic delusion, caused by the passions of desire and aversion, there cannot indeed arise a knowledge of things as they are, even of the external world; far less can such an intellect grasp the transcendental knowledge of the innermost Self.

28. Those men of virtuous deeds, whose sin has come to an end,—they, freed from the delusion of the pairs of opposites, worship Me with firm resolve.

29. Those who strive for freedom from old age and death, taking refuge in Me, they know. Brahman, the whole of Adhyâtma, and Karma in its entirety.[178]

30. Those who know Me with the Adhibhuta, the Adhidaiva, and the Adhiyajna, (continue to) know Me even at the time of death, steadfast in mind.[179]

EIGHTH CHAPTER
The Way to the Imperishable Brahman

Arjuna said:

1. What is that Brahman, what is Adhyâtma, what is Karma, O best of Purushas? What is called Adhibhuta, and what Adhidaiva?

2. Who, and in what way, is Adhiyajna here in this body, O destroyer of Madhu? And how art Thou known at the time of death, by the self-controlled?

The Blessed Lord said:

3. The Imperishable is the Supreme Brahman. Its dwelling in each individual body is called Adhyâtma; the offering in sacrifice which causes the genesis and support of beings, is called Karma.[180]

4. The perishable adjunct is the Adhibhuta, and the Indweller is the Adhidaivata; I alone am the Adhiyajna here in this body, O best of the embodied.[181]

---

178 (They know) the whole of Adhyâtma: They realise in full the Reality underlying the innermost individual Self.

179 Their consciousness of Me continues as ever, unaffected by the change of approaching death.

180 Offering in sacrifice—includes here all virtuous works.
Karma: Cf. III. 14, 15.

181 Adhibhuta: that perishable adjunct which is different from, and yet depends for its existence on the self-conscious principle, i.e., everything

5. And he, who at the time of death, meditating on Me alone, goes forth, leaving the body, attains My Being: there is no doubt about this.

6. Remembering whatever object, at the end, he leaves the body, that alone is reached by him, O son of Kunti, (because) of his constant thought of that object.[182]

7. Therefore, at all times, constantly remember Me, and fight. With mind and intellect absorbed, in Me, thou shalt doubtless come to Me.[183]

8. With the mind not moving towards anything else, made steadfast by the method of habitual meditation, and dwelling on the Supreme, Resplendent Purusha, O son of Prithâ, one goes to Him.[184]

9-10. The Omniscient, the Ancient, the Overruler, minuter than an atom, the Sustainer of all, of form inconceivable, self-luminous like the sun, and beyond the darkness of Mâyâ—he who meditates on Him thus, at the time of death, full of devotion, with the mind unmoving, and also by the power of Yoga, fixing the whole Prâna betwixt the eye-brows, he goes to that Supreme, Resplendent Purusha.[185]

11. What the knowers of the Veda speak of as Imperishable, what

---

material, everything that has birth.
Adhidaivata: The universal Self in Its subtle aspect: the Centre from which all living beings have their sense-power.
Adhiyajna: the presiding deity of sacrifice,—Vishnu.

182 Constant thought: the idea is, that the most prominent thought of one's life occupies the mind at the time of death. One cannot get rid of it, even as one cannot get rid of a disagreeable thought-image in a dream; so the character of the body to be next attained by one is determined accordingly, i.e., by the final thought.

183 Remember Me and fight: Do thou constantly keep thy mind fixed on Me and at the same time perform thy Swadharma, as befits a Kshatriya; and thus thou shalt attain purification of the heart.

184 Method—Yoga.
Resplendent—the Being in the solar orb, same as Adhidaivata, of the fourth sloka.

185 Self-luminous. Known by no agency like the understanding, the mind or the senses, but by Self alone.
Power of Yoga—which comes by the constant practice of Samâdhi.
Prâna: the vital current.
Fixing the whole Prâna—means, concentrating the whole will and self-consciousness.

the self-controlled (Sannyâsins), freed from attachment enter, and to gain which goal they live the life of a Brahmachârin, that I shall declare unto thee in brief.[186]

12-13. Controlling all the senses, confining the mind in the heart, drawing the Prâna into the head, occupied in the practice of concentration, uttering the one-syllabled "Om"—the Brahman, and meditating on Me;—he who so departs, leaving the body, attains the Supreme Goal.

14. I am easily attainable by that ever-steadfast Yogin who remembers Me constantly and daily, with a single mind, O son of Prithâ.

15. Reaching the highest perfection, and having attained Me, the great-souled ones are no more subject to re-birth—which is the home of pain, and ephemeral.[187]

16. All the worlds, O Arjuna, including the realm of Brahmâ, are subject to return, but after attaining Me, O son of Kunti, there is no re-birth. [188]

17. They who know (the true measure of) day and night, know the day of Brahmâ, which ends in a thousand Yugas, and the night which (also) ends in a thousand Yugas.[189]

18. At the approach of (Brahmâ's) day, all manifestations proceed from the unmanifested state; at the approach of night, they merge verily into that alone, which is called the unmanifested.

19. The very same multitude of beings (that existed in the preceding day of Brahmâ), being born again and again, merge, in spite of themselves, O son of Prithâ, (into the unmanifested), at the approach of night, and re-manifest at the approach of day.[190]

20. But beyond this unmanifested, there is that other Unmanifested,

186 Brahmachârin—a religious student who takes the vow of continence etc.; every moment of this stage is one of hard discipline and asceticism.

Cf. Kathopanishad, II. 14.

187 Ephemeral: non-eternal, of an ever-changing nature.

188 Subject to return—because limited by time.

189 Day and night—mean evolution and involution of the whole universe respectively.

190 Being born . . . themselves: They repeatedly come forth and dissolve, being forced by the effects of their own Karma.

Eternal Existence—That which is not destroyed at the destruction of all beings.[191]

21. What has been called Unmanifested and Imperishable, has been described as the Goal Supreme. That is My highest state, having attained which, there is no return.

22. And that Supreme Purusha is attainable, O son of Prithâ, by whole-souled devotion to Him alone, in Whom all beings dwell, and by Whom all this is pervaded.

23. Now I shall tell thee, O bull of the Bhâratas, of the time (path) travelling in which, the Yogis return, (and again of that, taking which) they do not return.

24. Fire, flame, day-time, the bright fortnight, the six months of the Northern passage of the sun, taking this path, the knowers of Brahman go to Brahman.

25. Smoke, night-time, the dark fortnight, the six months of the Southern passage of the sun—taking this path the Yogi, attaining the lunar light, returns.[192]

191 This unmanifested—which being the seed of the manifested, is Avidyâ itself.

192 It is difficult to decide the true significance of these two verses (24 & 25). Some are inclined to think that each of the steps means a sphere; while others, a state of consciousness. Still others think, that the series beginning with fire means developing states of illumination and renunciation, and that beginning with smoke, increasing states of ignorance and attachment.

The two paths, Devayâna and Pitriyâna, by which the souls of the dead are supposed to travel to the other world according to their deserts are mentioned in the Upanishads, prominently in the Chhândogya, V. x. I, 2. Bâdarâyana discusses these passages in the Brahma Sutras, IV. ii. 18-21. But an interesting light has been thrown upon the question by the late Mr. Tilak's theory of the Arctic home of the ancestors of the Aryan race. He has also dealt with his subject specially, in a paper of great value which appeared in Prabuddha Bharata (Vol. IX.). Considering the importance of the doctrine and the excellent way in which it has been elucidated by Mr. Tilak, we shall briefly note below the main heads of his argument.

The words Pitriyâna and Devayâna are used many times in the Rigveda. But the distinction made in the Upanishads about the soul's path, according as a man died during the dark or the bright half of the year, was unknown to the bards of the Rigveda, who held the view that the soul of a man always travelled by the Pitriyâna road, whatever the time of his death. It is therefore clear that

26. Truly are these bright and dark paths of the world considered eternal: one leads to non-return; by the other, one returns.[193]

27. No Yogi, O son of Prithâ, is deluded after knowing these paths. Therefore, O Arjuna, be thou steadfast in Yoga, at all times.[194]

28. Whatever meritorious effect is declared (in the Scriptures) to accrue from (the study of) the Vedas, (the performance of) Yajnas, (the practice of) austerities and gifts,—above all this rises the Yogi, having known this, and attains to the primeval, supreme Abode.[195]

---

the doctrine of the Upanishads was a later development, probably evolved after physical light and darkness had come to be connected with moral good and evil and the dual character of the world was established. Now, if along with this we consider that death during the Southern passage of the sun was regarded as inauspicious from the Arctic times, we can see how the distinction arose between the paths of a man's soul according as he died in the dark or the bright part of the year.

As to the series of steps in each path, since Agni was believed to be the only leader of the soul on its path, and both paths ended with the passages of the sun, the starting and halting points thus settled, it was not difficult to fill in the intermediate steps. The dual character of the world is manifested in Agni as flame and smoke. The flame was therefore the starting point of one path and smoke, of the other. Day and night, increasing and decreasing moon, Northern and Southern passages of the sun came next in natural order. The number of steps can easily be increased, and as a matter of fact has been increased in the Kaushitaki and some other Upanishads, on the same general principle.

Another point in this connection may be noted. There is nothing in the second or Pitriyâna path to correspond with Agni, in the first. We must therefore either reduce the number of steps in the first path by taking the words "fire" and "flame" in appositional relation and translate the same as "fire, that is flame," or increase the steps in the second by adding "fire" as one.

193 The paths are eternal, because Samsâra is eternal.

194 Knowing that one of the paths leads to Samsâra and the other to Moksha, the Yogi takes up the one leading to illumination and rejects the other

195 This—the truth imparted by the Lord in answer to the questions of Arjuna at the beginning of the present chapter.

NINTH CHAPTER
The Way of the Kingly Knowledge and the Kingly Secret

The Blessed Lord said:

1. To thee, who dost not carp, verily shall I now declare this, the most profound knowledge, united with realisation, having known which, thou shalt be free from evil (Samsâra).

2. Of sciences, the highest; of profundities, the deepest; of purifiers, the supreme, is this; realisable by direct perception, endowed with (immense) merit, very easy to perform, and of an imperishable nature.

3. Persons without Shraddhâ for this Dharma, return, O scorcher of foes, without attaining Me, to the path of re-birth fraught with death. [196]

4. All this world is pervaded by me in My unmanifested form: all beings exist in Me, but I do not dwell in them.[197]

5. Nor do beings exist in Me (in reality), behold My Divine Yoga! Bringing forth and supporting the beings, My Self does not dwell in them. [198]

6. As the mighty wind, moving always everywhere, rests ever in the Akâsha, know thou, that even so do all beings rest in Me.[199]

7. At the end of a Kalpa, O son of Kunti, all beings go back to My

---

196 Without . . . Dharma: Who have no faith in this knowledge of the Self, regarding the physical body itself as the Self.

197 Unmanifested: being invisible to the senses.

Exist in Me—have an individual existence through Me, the Self, underlying them all.

Do not dwell in them—like corporeal things—in contact with them, or contained as though in a receptacle.

198 Vide vii. 12.

Nor do &c.—Because of the Self Being unattached to or unconnected with any object. "Devoid of attachment. He is never attached."—Brih. Upa. III—ix-26.

199 Rests ever in the Akâsha—without being attached to it.

The idea is that beings rest in the Lord without contact with, and so without producing any effect on Him.

Prakriti: at the beginning of (another) Kalpa, I send them forth again.[200]

8. Animating My Prakriti, I project again and again this whole multitude of beings, helpless under the sway of Prakriti.[201]

9. These acts do not bind Me, sitting as one neutral, unattached to them, O Dhananjaya.[202]

10. By reason of My proximity, Prakriti produces all this, the moving and the unmoving; the world wheels round and round, O son of Kunti, because of this.[203]

11. Unaware of My higher state, as the great Lord of beings, fools disregard Me, dwelling in the human form.[204]

12. Of vain hopes, of vain works, of vain knowledge, and senseless, they verily are possessed of the delusive nature of Râkshasas and Asuras. [205]

---

200 Prakriti: The inferior one composed of the three Gunas.
Kalpa—a period of cosmic manifestation.

201 Animating My Prakriti—invigorating and fertilising the Prakriti dependent on Him, which had gone to sleep at the universal dissolution, at the end of the Kalpa.

202 These acts—which involve the unequal creation and dissolution of the universe.
As in the case of Ishvara, so in the case of others also, the absence of the egotistic feeling of agency and attachment for results, is the cause of freedom (from Dharma and Adharma).

203 In verses VII to X the Lord defines His position, following the Arundhati Nyâya. When a bride is brought to her husband's house for the first time, he shows her a very tiny star, called Arundhati. To do this, he has to direct her gaze the right way, which he does by asking her to look at something near and something big, in the direction of the star, e.g., a branch of a tree. Next, he draws her attention to a large bright star observed beyond this branch, and so on, till by several steps, he succeeds in leading her eyes to the right thing. This method of leading to a subtle object through easy steps, is called Arundhati Nyâya. The Lord begins by stating that He projects all beings at the beginning of evolution: Prakriti is only an instrument in His hands. Next, He says, He is not affected by that act, since He sits by, as one neutral, perfectly unattached. Lastly, He leads up to the final truth that really He does nothing, that it is Prakriti, who animated by His proximity produces all that is. It is His Light that lights up Prakriti, and makes her live and act. That is all the relation between Him and her.

204 Great Lord—Supreme Self.

205 Vain—because they neglect their own Self. They see no Self beyond

13. But the great-souled ones, O son of Prithâ, possessed of the Divine Prakriti, knowing Me to be the origin of beings, and immutable, worship Me with a single mind.[206]

14. Glorifying Me always and striving with firm resolve, bowing down to Me in devotion, always steadfast, they worship Me.

15. Others, too, sacrificing by the Yajna of knowledge (i.e., seeing the Self in all), worship Me the All-Formed, as one, as distinct, as manifold. [207]

16. I am the Kratu, I the Yajna, I the Svadhâ, I the Aushadham, I the Mantra, I the Ajyam, I the fire, and I the oblation.[208]

17. I am the Father of this world, the Mother, the Sustainer, the Grandfather; the Purifier, the (one) thing to be known, (the syllable) Om, and also the Rik, Sâman and Yajus.[209]

18. The Goal, the Supporter, the Lord, the Witness, the Abode, the Refuge, the Friend, the Origin, the Dissolution, the Substratum, the Storehouse, the Seed immutable.[210]

19. (As sun) I give heat: I withhold and send forth rain; I am immortality and also death; being and non-being am I, O Arjuna![211]

---

the body.

They—refers to those described in the preceding Sloka.

Râkshasas have Râjasika nature, Asuras, Tâmasika.

206 Divine: Sâttvika.

207 All-Formed: He who has assumed all the manifold forms in the universe.

As one—identifying himself with the All-Formed;—the Advaita view.

As distinct—making a distinction in essence between the Lord and himself:—the Dualistic view.

As manifold—as the various divinities, Brahma, Rudra &c.

208 Kratu is a particular Vedic rite.

Yajna: The worship enjoined in the Smriti.

Svadhâ: food offered to the manes (Pitris).

Aushadham: all vegetable food and medicinal herbs.

Mantra: the chant with which oblation is offered. Ajyam: articles of oblation.

The fire—into which the offering is poured.

209 Sustainer—by dispensing fruit of action.

210 Seed: cause of the origin of all things.

Immutable—because it endures so long as the Samsâra endures.

211 Being: The manifested world of effects.

Non-being—means, the cause which is unmanifested only, and not non-

20. The knowers of the three Vedas, worshipping Me by Yajna, drinking the Soma, and (thus) being purified from sin, pray for passage to heaven; reaching the holy world of the Lord of the Devas, they enjoy in heaven the divine pleasures of the Devas.[212]

21. Having enjoyed the vast Swarga-world, they enter the mortal world, on the exhaustion of their merit: Thus, abiding by the injunctions of the three (Vedas), desiring desires, they (constantly) come and go.[213]

22. Persons who, meditating on Me as non-separate, worship Me in all beings, to them thus ever jealously engaged, I carry what they lack and preserve what they already have.[214]

23. Even those devotees, who endued with Shraddhâ, worship other gods, they too worship Me alone, O son of Kunti, (but) by the wrong method.[215]

24. For I alone am the Enjoyer, and Lord of all Yajnas; but because they do not know Me in reality, they return, (to the mortal world).[216]

25. Votaries of the Devas go to the Devas; to the Pitris, go their votaries; to the Bhutas, go the Bhuta worshippers; My votaries too come unto Me.[217]

---

existence; otherwise we have to conceive existence coming out of nonexistence, which is absurd. The Sruti says, "How can existence come out of non-existence?"—Chhand. Upa. 6.

212 Lord of the Devas—Indra, who is called Satakratu, because he had performed a hundred sacrifices.

213 Injunctions—Ritualistic, the Karma-Kânda.

214 Ananyâh—as non-separate, i.e., looking upon the Supreme Being as not separate from their own self. Or Ananyâh may mean, without any other (thought). Then the translation of the Sloka should be—persons who worship Me in all beings, never harbouring any other thought, to them &c.

I carry &c.—Because while other devotees work for their own gain and safety, those who do not see anything as separate from themselves, do not do so; they even do not cherish a desire for life; so the Lord secures to them gain and safety.

215 Wrong method—ignorantly, not in the way by which they can get Moksha.

216 They return—by worshipping other gods they attain no doubt to the spheres of their sacrifice, but after the exhaustion of this merit, they fall from those spheres and return to the mortal world.

217 Bhutas—beings lower than the Devas, but higher than human beings.

26. Whoever with devotion offers Me a leaf, a flower, a fruit, or water, that I accept—the devout gift of the pure-minded.[218]

27. Whatever thou doest, whatever thou eatest, whatever thou offerest in sacrifice, whatever thou givest away, whatever austerity thou practisest, O son of Kunti, do that as an offering unto Me.

28. Thus shalt thou be freed from the bondages of actions, bearing good and evil results: with the heart steadfast in the Yoga of renunciation, and liberated, thou shalt come unto Me.[219]

29. I am the same to all beings: to Me there is none hateful or dear. But those who worship Me with devotion, are in Me, and I too am in them. [220]

30. If even a very wicked person worships Me, with devotion to none else, he should be regarded as good, for he has rightly resolved.[221]

31. Soon does he become righteous, and attain eternal Peace, O son of Kunti boldly canst thou proclaim, that My devotee is never destroyed.

32. For, taking refuge in Me, they also, O son of Prithâ, who might be of inferior birth,—women, Vaishyas, as well as Sudras,—even they attain to the Supreme Goal.[222]

Me—The Imperishable.

218 Not only does the single-minded devotion to the Supreme lead to imperishable result, but it is also so easy and simple to perform,—says Krishna in this Sloka.

219 The Yoga of renunciation—This way of purification of the heart by offering everything to the Lord.

Liberated &c.—thou shalt be liberated while in the body, and at its death, become Me.

220 I am like fire. As fire gives heat to those who draw near to it, and not to those who move away from it, even so do I. My grace falls upon My devotees, but not owing to any attachment on My part. As the sun's light, though pervading everywhere, is reflected in a clean mirror, so also I, the Supreme Lord, present as a matter of course everywhere, manifest Myself in those persons only, from whose minds all the dirt of ignorance has been removed by devotion.

221 He has rightly resolved—He is one who has formed a holy resolution, to abandon the evil ways of his life.

222 Of inferior birth . . . Sudras—Because by birth, the Vaishyas are engaged only in agriculture &c., and the women and Sudras are debarred from the study of the Vedas.

33. What need to mention holy Brâhmanas, and devoted Râjarshis! Having obtained this transient, joyless world, worship thou Me.[223]

34. Fill thy mind with Me, be My devotee, sacrifice unto Me, bow down to Me; thus having made thy heart steadfast in Me, taking Me as the Supreme Goal, thou shalt come to Me.

TENTH CHAPTER
Glimpses of the Divine Glory

The Blessed Lord said:

1. Again, O mighty-armed, do thou listen to My supreme word, which I, wishing thy welfare, will tell thee who art delighted (to hear Me).[224]

2. Neither the hosts of Devas, nor the great Rishis, know My origin, for in every way I am the source of all the Devas and the great Rishis.[225]

3. He who knows Me, birthless and beginningless, the great Lord of worlds—he, among mortals, is undeluded, he is freed from all sins.[226]

4-5. Intellect, knowledge, non-delusion, forbearance, truth, restraint of the external senses, calmness of heart, happiness, misery, birth, death, fear, as well as fearlessness, non-injury, evenness, contentment, austerity, benevolence, good name, (as well as) ill-fame;—(these) different kinds of qualities of beings arise from Me alone.[227]

---

223 Râjarshis—kings who have attained to sainthood (Rishihood).
What need &c.: How much more easily then do the holy Brâhmanas and the devoted royal saints attain that Goal!
Having . . . world—Being born in this human body which is hard to get, one should exert oneself immediately for perfection, without depending on the future, as everything in this world is transient, and without seeking for happiness, as this world is joyless.

224 Supreme—as revealing the unsurpassed truth.

225 Prabhavam—higher origin (birth);—though birthless, yet taking various manifestations of power. Or it may mean, great Lordly power.
In every way: not only as their producer, but also as their efficient cause, and the guide of their intellect, &c.

226 All sins—consciously or unconsciously incurred.

227 Arise &c.—according to their respective Karma.

6. The seven great Rishis as well as the four ancient Manus, possessed of powers like Me (due to their thoughts being fixed on Me), were born of (My) mind; from them are these creatures in the world.[228]

7. He who in reality knows these manifold manifestations of My being and (this) Yoga power of Mine, becomes established in the unshakable Yoga; there is no doubt about it.[229]

8. I am the origin of all, from Me everything evolves;—thus thinking the wise worship Me with loving consciousness.[230]

9. With their minds wholly in Me, with their senses absorbed in Me, enlightening one another, and always speaking of Me, they are satisfied and delighted.[231]

10. To them, ever steadfast and serving Me with affection, I give that Buddhi Yoga by which they come unto Me.[232]

11. Out of mere compassion for them,

I, abiding in their hearts, destroy the darkness (in them) born of ignorance, by the luminous lamp of knowledge.[233]

---

228 The four ancient Manus: The four Manus of the past ages known as Savarnas.

229 This Yoga power—i.e., the fact that the great Rishis and the Manus possessed their power and wisdom, as partaking of a very small portion of the Lord's infinite power and wisdom.

Unshakable Yoga: Samâdhi, the state of steadiness in right realisation.

230 Loving consciousness—of the One Self in all.

231 Satisfied: when there is cessation of all thirst.

Says the Purâna: All the pleasures of the senses in the world, and also all the great happiness in the divine spheres, are not worth a sixteenth part of that which comes from the cessation of all desires.

232 Buddhi Yoga—Devotion of right knowledge, through Dhyâna, of My essential nature as devoid of all limitations. See II. 39.

233 Luminous lamp of knowledge—characterised by discrimination; fed by the oil of contentment due to Bhakti; fanned by the wind of absorbing meditation on Me; furnished with the wick of pure consciousness evolved by the constant cultivation of Brahmacharyam and other pious virtues; held in the reservoir of the heart devoid of worldliness; placed in the wind-sheltered recess of the mind, withdrawn from the sense-objects, and untainted by attachment and aversion; shining with the light of right knowledge, engendered by incessant practice of concentration.—Sankara.

Arjuna said:

12-13. The Supreme Brahman, the Supreme Abode, the Supreme Purifier, art Thou. All the Rishis, the Deva-Rishi Nârada as well as Asita, Devala and Vyâsa have declared Thee as the Eternal, the Self-luminous Purusha, the first Deva, Birth-less and All-pervading. So also Thou Thyself sayest to me.

14. I regard all this that Thou sayest to me as true, O Keshava. Verily, O Bhagavân, neither the Devas nor the Dânavas know Thy manifestation. [234]

15. Verily, Thou Thyself knowest Thyself by Thyself, O Purusha Supreme, O Source of beings, O Lord of beings, O Deva of Devas, O Ruler of the world.

16. Thou shouldst indeed speak, without reserve, of Thy divine attributes by which, filling all these worlds, Thou existest.[235]

17. How shall I, O Yogin, meditate ever to know Thee? In what things, Bhagavân, art Thou to be thought of by me?[236]

18. Speak to me again in detail, Jnanârdana, of Thy Yoga-powers and attributes; for I am never satiated in hearing the ambrosia (of Thy speech). [237]

The Blessed Lord said:

19. I shall speak to thee now, O best of the Kurus, of My divine attributes, according to their prominence; there is no end to the particulars of My manifestation.[238]

20. I am the Self, O Gudâkesha, existent in the heart of all beings; I

---

234 Bhagavân—is he in whom ever exist in their fulness, all powers, all Dharma, all glory, all success, all renunciation and all freedom. Also he that knows the origin and dissolution and the future of all beings, as well as knowledge and ignorance, is called Bhagavân.

235 Since none else can do so.

236 In what things &c.: In order that the mind even thinking of external objects, may be enabled to contemplate Thee in Thy particular manifestations in them.

237 Janârdana—to whom all pray for prosperity and salvation.

238 According to their prominence, i.e., only where they are severally the most prominent.

am the beginning, the middle, and also the end of all beings.[239]

21. Of the Adityas, I am Vishnu; of luminaries, the radiant Sun; of the winds, I am Marichi; of the asterisms, the Moon.

22. I am the Sâma-Veda of the Vedas, and Vâsava (Indra) of the gods; of the senses I am Manas, and intelligence in living beings am I.

23. And of the Rudras I am Sankara, of the Yakshas and Râkshasas the Lord of wealth (Kuvera), of the Vasus I am Pâvaka, and of mountains, Meru am I.

24. And of priests, O son of Prithâ, know Me the chief, Brihaspati; of generals, I am Skanda; of bodies of water, I am the ocean.

25. Of the great Rishis I am Bhrigu; of words I am the one syllable "Om"; of Yajnas I am the Yajna of Japa (silent repetition); of immovable things the Himâlaya.[240]

26. Of all trees (I am) the Ashvattha, and Nârada of Deva-Rishis; Chitraratha of Gandharvas am I, and the Muni Kapila of the perfected ones.

27. Know Me among horses as Uchchaisshravas, Amrita-born; of lordly elephants Airâvata, and of men the king.[241]

28. Of weapons I am the thunderbolt, of cows I am Kâmadhuk; I am the Kandarpa, the cause of offspring; of serpents I am Vâsuki.

29. And Ananta of snakes I am, I am Varuna of water-beings; and Aryaman of Pitris I am, I am Yama of controllers.

30. And Prahlâda am I of Diti's progeny, of measurers I am Time; and of beasts I am the lord of beasts, and Garuda of birds.

31. Of purifiers I am the wind, Râma of warriors am I; of fishes I am the shark, of streams I am Jâhnavi (the Ganges).

32. Of manifestations I, am the beginning, the middle and also the

239 Gudâkesha—conqueror of sleep.
Beginning etc.—That is, the birth, the life, and the death of all beings.

240 Yajna of Japa—because there is no injury or loss of life involved in it, it is the best of all Yajnas.

241 Amrita-born: Brought forth from the ocean when it was churned for the nectar.

end; of all knowledges I am the knowledge of the Self, and Vâda of disputants.[242]

33. Of letters the letter A am I, and Dvandva of all compounds; I alone am the inexhaustible Time, I the Sustainer (by dispensing fruits of actions) All-formed.[243]

34. And I am the all-seizing Death, and the prosperity of those who are to be prosperous; of the feminine qualities (I am) Fame, Prosperity (or beauty), Inspiration, Memory, Intelligence, Constancy and Forbearance.

35. Of Sâmas also I am the Brihat-Sâma, of metres Gâyatri am I; of months I am Mârgashirsha, of seasons the flowery season.[244]

36. I am the gambling of the fraudulent, I am the power of the powerful; I am victory, I am effort, I am Sattva of the Sâttvika.[245]

37. Of the Vrishnis I am Vâsudeva; of the Pândavas, Dhananjaya; and also of the Munis I am Vyâsa; of the sages, Ushanas the sage.

38. Of punishers I am the sceptre; of those who seek to conquer, I am statesmanship; and also of things secret I am silence, and the knowledge of knowers am I.

39. And whatsoever is the seed of all beings, that also am I, O Arjuna. There is no being, whether moving or unmoving, that can exist without Me.

40. There is no end of My divine attributes, O scorcher of foes; but this is a brief statement by Me of the particulars of My divine attributes.

41. Whatever being there is great, prosperous or powerful, that know thou to be a product of a part of My splendour.

---

242 Vâda. Discussion is classified under three heads: 1. Vâda; 2. Vitandâ; 3. Jalpa.
In the first, the object is to arrive at truth; in the second, idle carping at the arguments of another, without trying to establish the opposite side of the question; and in the third, the assertion of one's own opinion, and the attempt to refute that of the adversary by overbearing reply or wrangling rejoinder.

243 Inexhaustible Time, i.e., Eternity. Kâla spoken of before is finite time.

244 Mârgashirsha—month including parts of November and December. Flowery season—Spring.

245 I am victory, I am effort: I am victory of the victorious, I am the effort of those who make an effort.

42. Or what avails thee to know all this diversity, O Arjuna? (Know thou this,. that) I exist, supporting this whole world by a portion of Myself.

ELEVENTH CHAPTER
The Vision of the Universal Form

Arjuna said:

1. By the supremely profound words, on the discrimination of Self, that have been spoken by Thee out of compassion towards me, this my delusion is gone.

2. Of Thee, O lotus-eyed, I have heard at length, of the origin and dissolution of beings, as also Thy inexhaustible greatness.

3. So it is, O Lord Supreme! as Thou hast declared Thyself. (Still) I desire to see Thy Ishvara-Form, O Purusha Supreme.[246]

4. If, O Lord, Thou thinkest me capable of seeing it, then, O Lord of Yogis, show me Thy immutable Self.

The Blessed Lord said:

5. Behold, O son of Prithâ, by hundreds and thousands, My different forms celestial, of various colours and shapes.

6. Behold the Adityas, the Vasus, the Rudras, the twin Ashvins, and the Maruts; behold, O descendant of Bharata, many wonders never seen before.

7. See now, O Gudâkesha, in this My body, the whole universe centred in one,—including the moving and the unmoving,—and all else that thou desirest to see.[247]

8. But thou canst not see Me with these eyes of thine; I give thee

---

246 Thy Ishvara-Form—as possessed of omnipotence, omnipresence, infinite wisdom, strength, virtue and splendour.

247 Centred in one—as part of My body.
All else—e.g., your success or defeat in the war, about which you entertain a doubt (II. 6).

supersensuous sight; behold My Yoga Power Supreme.[248]

Sanjaya said:

9. Having thus spoken, O King, Hari, the Great Lord of Yoga, showed unto the son of Prithâ, His Supreme Ishvara-Form—

10. With numerous mouths and eyes, with numerous wondrous sights, with numerous celestial ornaments, with numerous celestial weapons uplifted;

11. Wearing celestial garlands and apparel, anointed with celestial-scented unguents, the All-wonderful, Resplendent, Boundless and All-formed.

12. If the splendour of a thousand suns were to rise up at once in the sky, that would be like the splendour of that Mighty Being.[249]

13. There in the body of the God of gods, the son of Pându then saw the whole universe resting in one, with its manifold divisions.

14. Then Dhananjaya, filled with wonder, with his hair standing on end, bending down his head to the Deva in adoration, spoke with joined palms.[250]

Arjuna said:

15. I see all the Devas, O Deva, in Thy body, and hosts of all grades of beings; Brahma, the Lord, seated on the lotus, and all the Rishis and celestial serpents.

16. I see Thee of boundless form on every side with manifold arms, stomachs, mouths and eyes; neither the end nor the middle, nor also the beginning of Thee do I see, O Lord of the universe, O Universal Form.

17. I see Thee with diadem, club, and discus; a mass of radiance shining everywhere, very hard to look at, all around blazing like burning fire and sun, and immeasurable.

---

248 Me—in My Universal Form.

249 Mighty Being: The Universal Form.
The splendour of the Universal Form excels all others; it is indeed beyond compare.

250 Deva: God, in His Universal Form.

18. Thou art the Imperishable, the Supreme Being, the one thing to be known. Thou art the great Refuge of this universe;. Thou art the undying Guardian of the Eternal Dharma, Thou art the Ancient. Purusha, I ween.

19. I see Thee without beginning, middle or end, infinite in power, of manifold arms; the sun and the moon Thine eyes, the burning fire Thy mouth; heating the whole universe with Thy radiance.

20. The space betwixt heaven and earth and all the quarters are filled by Thee alone; having seen this, Thy marvellous and awful Form, the three worlds are trembling with fear, O Great-souled One.

21. Verily, into Thee enter these hosts of Devas; some extol Thee in fear with joined palms; "May it be well!" thus saying, bands of great Rishis and Siddhas praise Thee with splendid hymns.

22. The Rudras, Adityas, Vasus, Sâdhyas, Vishva-Devas, the two Ashvins, Maruts, Ushmapâs, and hosts of Gandharvas, Yakshas, Asuras, and Siddhas,—all these are looking at Thee, all quite astounded.[251]

23. Having seen Thy immeasurable Form—with many mouths and eyes, O mighty-armed, with many arms. thighs and feet, with many stomachs, and fearful with many tusks,—the worlds are terrified, and so am I.

24. On seeing Thee touching the sky, shining in many a colour, with mouths wide open, with large fiery eyes, I am terrified at heart, and find no courage nor peace, O Vishnu.

25. Having seen Thy mouths, fearful with tusks, (blazing) like Pralaya-fires, I know not the four quarters, nor do I find peace; have mercy, O Lord of the Devas, O Abode of the universe.[252]

26-27. All these sons of Dhritarâshtra, with hosts of monarchs, Bhishma, Drona, and Sutaputra, with the warrior chiefs of ours, enter precipitately into Thy mouth, terrible with tusks and fearful to behold. Some are found sticking in the interstices of Thy teeth, with their heads crushed to powder.[253]

---

251 Ushmapâs—The Pitris.

252 Pralaya-fires: The fires which consume the worlds at the time of the final dissolution (Pralaya) of the universe

I know . . . quarters: I cannot distinguish the East from the West, nor the North from the South.

253 Sutaputra: The son of a charioteer, Kama.

28. Verily, as the many torrents of rivers flow towards the ocean, so do these heroes in the world of men enter Thy fiercely flaming mouths.28

29. As moths precipitately rush into a blazing fire only to perish, even so do these creatures also precipitately rush into Thy mouths only to perish.[254]

30. Swallowing all the worlds on every side with Thy flaming mouths, Thou are licking Thy lips. Thy fierce rays, filling the whole world with radiance, are burning, O Vishnu![255]

31. Tell me who Thou art, fierce in form. Salutation to Thee, O Deva Supreme; have mercy. I desire to know Thee, O Primeval One. I know not indeed Thy purpose.

The Blessed Lord said:

32. I am the mighty world-destroying Time, here made manifest for the purpose of infolding the world. Even without thee, none of the warriors arrayed in the hostile armies shall live.[256]

33. Therefore do thou arise and acquire fame. Conquer the enemies, and enjoy the unrivalled dominion. Verily by Myself have they been already slain; be thou merely an apparent cause, O Savyasâchin (Arjuna). [257]

34. Drona, Bhishma, Jayadratha, Karna, as well as other brave warriors,—these already killed by Me, do thou kill. Be not distressed with fear; fight, and thou shalt conquer thy enemies in battle.[258]

---

254 28 & 29.—The two similes vividly illustrate how the assembled warriors rush to destruction, out of their uncontrollable nature, with or without discrimination.

255 Licking Thy lips: consuming entirely, enjoying it, as it were.

256 Even without thee &c.—Even without thy instrumentality, i.e., even if thou, O Arjuna, wouldst not fight, the end of all these warriors is inevitable, because I as the all-destroying Time have already killed them; so thy instrumentality in that work is insignificant.

257 Be thou . . . cause.—People will think thee as the vanquisher of thy enemies, whom even the Devas cannot kill, and thus thou wilt gain glory; but thou art only an instrument in My hand.
Savyasâchin—one who could shoot arrows even with his left hand.

258 Already killed by me:—so do not be afraid of incurring sin by killing Drona, Bhishma and others though they are venerable to you as; your Guru, grandsire, etc.

Sanjaya said:

35. Having, heard that speech of Keshava, the diademed one (Arjuna), with joined palms, trembling, prostrated himself, and again addressed Krishna in a choked voice, bowing down, overwhelmed with fear.

Arjuna said:

36. It is meet, O Hrishikesha, that the world is delighted and rejoices in Thy praise, that Râkshasas fly in fear to all quarters and all the hosts of Siddhas bow down to Thee in adoration.

37. And why should they not, O Great-souled One, bow to Thee, greater than, and the Primal Cause of even Brahmâ, O Infinite Being, O Lord of the Devas, O Abode of the universe? Thou art the Imperishable, the Being and the non-Being, (as well as) That which is Beyond (them). [259]

38. Thou art the Primal Deva, the Ancient Purusha; Thou art the Supreme Refuge of this universe, Thou art the Knower, and the One Thing to be known; Thou art the Supreme Goal. By Thee is the universe pervaded, O Boundless Form.

39. Thou art Vâyu, Yama, Agni, Varuna, the Moon, Prajâpati, and the Great-Grandfather. Salutation, salutation to Thee, a thousand times, and again and again salutation, salutation to Thee![260]

40. Salutation to Thee before and behind, salutation to Thee on every side, O All! Thou, infinite in power and infinite in prowess, pervadest all; wherefore Thou art All.[261]

41-42. Whatever I have presumptuously said from carelessness or

---

Distressed with fear—as regards success because these great warriors are regarded as invincible.

259 Brahmâ: the Hiranyagarbha.
The Being and the non-Being, &c.—The Sat (manifested) and the Asat (unmanifested), which form the Upâdhis (adjuncts) of the Akshara (Imperishable); as such He is spoken of as the Sat and the Asat. In reality, the Imperishable transcends the Sat and the Asat.

260 Vâyu . . . Moon: The God of wind, death, fire, waters, and the moon.
The Great-Grandfather—The Creator even of Brahmâ who is known as the Grandfather.

261 On every side: As Thou art present everywhere.
Pervadest: by Thy One Self.

love, addressing Thee as, "O Krishna, O Yâdava, O friend," regarding Thee merely as a friend, unconscious of this Thy greatness—in whatever way I may have been disrespectful to Thee in fun, while walking, reposing, sitting, or at meals, when alone (with Thee), O Achyuta, or in company—I implore Thee, Immeasurable One, to forgive all this.[262]

43. Thou art the Father of the world, moving and unmoving; the object of its worship; greater than the great. None there exists who is equal to Thee in the three worlds; who then can excel Thee, O. Thou of power incomparable?[263]

44. So prostrating my body in adoration, I crave Thy forgiveness, Lord adorable! As a father forgiveth his son, friend a dear friend, a beloved one his love, even so shouldst Thou forgive me, O Deva.

45. Overjoyed am I to have seen what I saw never before; yet my mind is distracted with terror. Show me, O Deva, only that Form of Thine. Have mercy, O Lord of Devas, O Abode of the universe.

46. Diademed, bearing a mace and a discus, Thee I desire to see as before. Assume that same four-armed Form, O Thou of thousand arms, of universal Form.

The Blessed Lord said:

47. Graciously have I shown to thee, O Arjuna, this Form supreme, by My own Yoga power, this resplendent, primeval, infinite, universal Form of Mine, which hath not been seen before by anyone else.

48. Neither by the study of the Veda and Yajna, nor by gifts, nor by rituals, nor by severe austerities, am I in such Form seen, in the world of men, by any other than thee, O great hero of the Kurus.

49. Be not afraid nor bewildered, having beheld this Form of Mine, so terrific. With thy fears dispelled and with gladdened heart, now see again this (former) form of Mine.

Sanjaya said:

---

262 Love: Confidence born of affection.
In company: in the presence of others.

263 None . . . to Thee—There cannot be two or more Ishvaras; if there were, the world could not get on as it does. When one Ishvara desires to create, another may desire to destroy. Who knows that all the different Ishvaras would be of one mind, as they would all be independent of each other?

50. So Vâsudeva, having thus spoken to Arjuna, showed again His own Form and the Great-souled One, assuming His gentle Form, pacified him who was terrified.

Arjuna said:

51. Having seen this Thy gentle human Form, O Janârdana, my thoughts are now composed and I am restored to my nature.

The Blessed Lord said:

52. Very hard indeed it is to see this Form of Mine which thou hast seen. Even the Devas ever long to behold this Form.

53. Neither by the Vedas, nor by austerity, nor by gifts, nor by sacrifice can I be seen as thou hast seen Me.

54. But by the single-minded devotion I may in this Form, be known, O Arjuna, and seen in reality, and also entered into, O scorcher of foes. [264]

55. He who does work for Me alone and has Me for his goal, is devoted to Me, is freed from attachment, and bears enmity towards no creature—he entereth into Me, O Pândava.[265]

TWELFTH CHAPTER
The Way of Devotion

Arjuna said:

1. Those devotees who, ever-steadfast, thus worship Thee, and those also who worship the Imperishable, the Unmanifested,—which of them

---

264 Single-minded devotion: That devotion which never seeks any other object but the Lord alone, and consequently cognises no other object but the Lord.

265 Does work for Me alone: Serves Me alone in all forms and manner of ways, with his whole heart and soul, and thus does not become attached to them.
He alone, whose devotion takes the forms as described in this sloka, can know and realise Him as He is in reality, and subsequently become one with Him.

are better versed in Yoga?[266]

The Blessed Lord said:

2. Those who, fixing their mind on Me, worship Me, ever-steadfast, and endowed with supreme Shraddhâ, they in My opinion are the best versed in Yoga.

3-4. But those also, who worship the Imperishable, the Indefinable, the Unmanifested, the Omnipresent, the Unthinkable, the Unchangeable, the Immovable, the Eternal,—having subdued all the senses, even-minded everywhere, engaged in the welfare of all beings, verily, they reach only Myself.[267]

5. Greater is their trouble whose minds are set on the Unmanifested; for the goal of the Unmanifested is very hard for the embodied to reach. [268]

6-7. But those who worship Me, resigning all actions in Me, regarding Me as the Supreme Goal, meditating on Me with single-minded Yoga,—to these whose mind is set on Me, verily, I become ere long, O son of Prithâ, the Saviour out of the ocean of the mortal Samsâra.[269]

8. Fix thy mind on Me only, place thy intellect in Me: (then) thou shalt no doubt live in Me hereafter.[270]

---

266 Thus: as declared in the last preceding verse (xi. 55).
The Unmanifested—Avyaktam—i.e., That which is incomprehensible to the senses, as devoid of all Upâdhis (see endnote).

267 Worship—Upâsanâ—is approaching the object of worship by way of meditating on it, in accordance with the teachings of the Shâstras and the Guru, and dwelling steadily in the current of that one thought, even as a thread of oil poured from one vessel to another.
Unchangeable—Kutastha: lit., remaining like a mass. He who is seated in Mâyâ as its Witness.

268 The embodied—Those who are attached to, or have identified themselves with, their bodies.
No comparison between the worshippers of the qualified and unqualified Brahman is meant here—since by the context, both reach the same goal. The path of the qualified Brahman is described as superior only because it is easier. The path of the unqualified Brahman is harder, because of the necessity of having to abandon all attachment to the body, from the very beginning of the practice.

269 Mortal Samsâra: The round of birth and death.

270 Mind—Manas: purpose and thought.
Intellect—the faculty which resolves and determines.

9. If thou art unable to fix thy mind steadily on Me, then by Abhyâsa-Yoga do thou seek to reach Me, O Dhananjaya.[271]

10. If also thou art unable to practise Abhyâsa, be thou intent on doing actions -for My sake. Even by doing actions for My sake, thou shalt attain perfection.

11. If thou art unable to do even this, then taking refuge in Me, abandon the fruit of all action, self-controlled.[272]

12. Better indeed is knowledge than (blind) Abhyâsa; meditation (with knowledge) is more esteemed than (mere) knowledge; than meditation the renunciation of the fruit of action; peace immediately follows renunciation.[273]

13-14. He who hates no creature, and is friendly and compassionate towards all, who is free from the feelings of 'I and mine,' even-minded in pain and pleasure, forbearing, ever content, steady in meditation, self-controlled, and possessed of firm conviction, with mind and intellect fixed on Me,—he who is thus devoted to Me, is dear to Me.

15. He by whom the world is not agitated and who cannot be agitated by the world, who is freed from joy, envy, fear and anxiety,—he is dear to Me.

16. He who is free from dependence, who is pure, prompt, uncon-

---

Live in Me—as My Self.

271 Abhyâsa-Yoga: the practice of repeatedly withdrawing the mind from the objects to which it wanders, and trying to fix it on one thing.

272 In the preceding Slokas,—first, the concentration of the mind on the Lord is enjoined; in case of inability to do that, Abhyâsa-Yoga is advised; if one finds that to be too hard, the performance of actions for the sake of the Lord alone, has been taught. Those who cannot do this even, who want to do things impelled by personal or other desires, are directed to give up the fruits of those actions to the Lord—i.e., not to anticipate, dwell or build on, or care for, the results, knowing them to be dependent upon the Lord. Those who cannot control their desire for work are taught to practise: indifference to the effects thereof.

273 Renunciation of the fruit of all action, as a means to the attainment of Bliss, is merely extolled here by the declaration of the superiority of one over another. Wherefore? Because it constitutes a common factor which immediately precedes Peace, both in the case of the man of wisdom who is steadily engaged in devout contemplation, and also of the ignorant one who, unable to tread the paths taught before, takes it up as the easiest means to Bliss.

cerned, untroubled, renouncing every undertaking,—he who is thus devoted to Me, is dear to Me.[274]

17. He who neither rejoices, nor hates, nor grieves, nor desires, renouncing good and evil, full of devotion, he is dear to Me.[275]

18-19. He who is the same to friend and foe, and also in honour and dishonour; who is the same in heat and cold, and in pleasure and pain; who is free from attachment; to whom censure and praise are equal; who is silent, content with anything, homeless, steady-minded, full of devotion,—that man is dear to Me.[276]

20. And they who follow this Immortal Dharma, as described above, endued with Shraddhâ, regarding Me as the Supreme Goal, and devoted,—they are exceedingly dear to Me.

THIRTEENTH CHAPTER
The Discrimination of the Kshetra and the Kshetra-jna

Arjuna said:

Prakriti and Purusha, also the Kshetra and the knower of the Kshetra, knowledge, and that which ought to be known—these, O Keshava, I desire to learn.[277]

The Blessed Lord said:

---

274 Free from dependence—on the body, the senses, the sense-objects, and their mutual connections.
Prompt: able to decide rightly and immediately in matters demanding prompt action.
Every undertaking—calculated to secure objects of desire, whether of this world or of the next.
275 Hates: Frets at receiving anything undesirable.
Grieves—at parting with a beloved object.
Desires—the unattained.
276 Content with anything, homeless: content with the bare means of bodily sustenance. Says the Mahabharata,—
"Who is clad with anything, who is fed on any food, who lies down anywhere, him the gods call a Brâhman."—Shanti Parva.
277 This verse is omitted in many editions.

1. This body, O son of Kunti, is called Kshetra, and he who knows it is called Kshetrajna by those who know of them (Kshetra and Kshetrajna).[278]

2. Me do thou also know, O descendant of Bharata, to be Kshetrajna in all Kshetras. The knowledge of Kshetra and Kshetrajna is considered by Me to be the knowledge.

3. What the Kshetra is, what its properties are, what are its modifications, what effects arise from what causes, and also who He is and what His powers are, that hear from Me in brief.[279]

4. (This truth) has been sung by Rishis in many ways, in various distinctive chants, in passages indicative of Brahman, full of reasoning, and convincing.

5-6. The great Elements, Egoism, Intellect, as also the Unmanifested (Mulâ Prakriti), the ten senses and the one (mind), and the five objects of the senses; desire, hatred, pleasure, pain, the, aggregate, intelligence, fortitude,—the Kshetra has been thus briefly described with its modifications.[280]

7. Humility, unpretentiousness, non-injury, forbearance, uprightness, service to the teacher, purity, steadiness, self-control;[281]

278 Kshetra: Literally, field; the body is so called because the fruits of action are reaped in it as in a field.

279 That: the true nature of Kshetra and Kshetrajna in all these specific aspects.

280 The Sânkhyas speak of those mentioned in the fifth Sloka as the twenty-four Tattvas or Principles.

The great Elements—Mahâbhutas—pervade all Vikâras, or modifications of matter.

Aggregate—Samghâta: combination of the body and the senses. p. 292

Desire and other qualities which the Vaiseshikas speak of as inherent attributes of the Atman, are spoken of in the sixth Sloka as merely the attributes of Kshetra, and not the attributes of Kshetrajna. Desire and other qualities mentioned here, stand for all the qualities of the Antah-Karana or inner sense,—as mere mental states. Each of them, being knowable, is Kshetra.

The Kshetra, of which the various modifications in their totality are spoken of as "this body" in the first Sloka, has been here dwelt upon in all its different forms, from 'The great Elements' to 'fortitude.'

281 Achârya—one who teaches the means of attaining Moksha.

8. The renunciation of sense-objects, and also absence of egoism; reflection on the evils of birth, death, old age, sickness and pain;[282]

9. Non-attachment, non-identification of self with son, wife, home, and the rest, and constant even-mindedness in the occurrence of the desirable and the un-undesirable;[283]

10. Unswerving devotion to Me by the Yoga of non-separation, resort to sequestered places, distaste for the society of men;[284]

11. Constant application to spiritual knowledge, understanding of the end of true knowledge: this is declared to be knowledge, and what is opposed to it is ignorance.[285]

12. I shall describe that which has to be known, knowing which one attains to immortality, the beginningless Supreme Brahman. It is called neither being nor non-being.

13. With hands and feet everywhere, with eyes, heads and mouths everywhere, with ears everywhere in the universe,—That exists pervad-

---

Purity—external and internal. The former consists in washing away the dirt from the body by means of water &c., and the latter—the purity of p. 293 mind—consists in the removal from it the dirt of attachment and other passions, by the recognition of evil in all objects of the senses.

282 Sense-objects: such as sound, touch &c., of pleasures seen or unseen. Pain—whether Adhyâtmic, i.e., arising in one's own person, or Adhibhautic, i.e., produced by external agents, or Adhidaivic, i.e., produced by supernatural beings.

Reflection . . . pain—or the passage may be interpreted as—reflection on the evils and miseries of birth, death, old age and sickness. Birth &c., are all miseries, not that they are miseries in themselves, but because they produce misery. From such reflection arises indifference to sense-pleasures, and the senses turn towards the Innermost Self for knowledge.

283 Identification of self—as in the case of a person who feels happy or miserable when another to whom he is attached, is happy or miserable, and who feels himself alive or dead when his beloved one is alive or dead.

284 Resort . . . places—favourable to equanimity of mind, so that uninterrupted meditation on the Self, . and the like, may be possible.

Society of men: of the unenlightened and undisciplined people, not of the pure and holy, because association with the latter leads to Jnâna.

285 These attributes—from 'Humility' to 'Understanding of the end of true knowledge'—are declared to be knowledge, because they are the means conducive to knowledge.

ing all.

14. Shining by the functions of all the senses, yet without the senses; Absolute, yet sustaining all; devoid of Gunas, yet their experiencer.

15. Without and within (all) beings; the unmoving and also the moving; because of Its subtlety incomprehensible; It is far and near.[286]

16. Impartible, yet It exists as if divided in beings: It is to be known as sustaining beings; and devouring, as well as generating (them).[287]

17. The Light even of lights, It is said to be beyond darkness; Knowledge, and the One Thing to be known, the Goal of' knowledge, dwelling in the hearts of all.[288]

18. Thus Kshetra, knowledge, and that which has to be known, have been briefly stated. Knowing this, My devotee is fitted for My state.

19. Know thou that Prakriti and Purusha are both beginningless; and know thou also that all modifications and Gunas are born of Prakriti.[289]

20. In the production of the body and the senses, Prakriti is said to be the cause; in the experience of pleasure and pain, Purusha is said to be the cause.[290]

21. Purusha seated in Prakriti, experiences the Gunas born of Prakriti; the reason of his birth in good and evil wombs is his attachment to the Gunas.[291]

---

286 Incomprehensible—to the unillumined, though knowable in Itself.
Far—when unknown.
Near—to the illumined, because It is their own Self.

287 Devouring—at the time of Pralaya.
Generating—at the time of utpatti or origin of the universe.

288 The Light even of lights:—The illuminator of all illuminating things, such as the sun &c., and Buddhi &c. Indeed, these latter shine only when illuminated by the Light of the consciousness of the Self.

289 Modifications—Vikâras: From Buddhi down to the physical body.

290 Senses—five organs of perception, five of action, mind, intellect and egoism.
Purusha: the Jiva is meant here.
Kârya: The effect, the physical body. Karana: Senses. Some read Kârana, and explain 'Kârya and Kârana' as 'effect and cause.'

291 Seated in: identifying himself with Gunas—manifesting themselves as pleasure, pain and delusion.

22. And the Supreme Purusha in this body is also called the Looker-on, the Permitter, the Supporter, the Experiencer, the Great Lord, and the Highest Self.[292]

23. He who thus knows the Purusha and Prakriti together with the Gunas, whatever his life, is not born again.[293]

24. Some by meditation behold the Self in their own intelligence by the purified heart, others by the path of knowledge, others again by Karma Yoga.

25. Others again not knowing thus, worship as they have heard from others. Even these go beyond death, regarding what they have heard as the Supreme Refuge.[294]

26. Whatever being is born, the moving or the unmoving, O bull of the Bhâratas, know it to be from the union of Kshetra and Kshetrajna.[295]

27. He sees, who sees the Lord Supreme, existing equally in all beings, deathless in the dying.

292 Looker-on, the Permitter—He himself does not participate in the activities of the bodily organs, the mind and the Buddhi, being quite apart from them, yet appears to be so engaged. And being a looker-on, He never stands in the way of the activities of Prakriti as manifested in the body. Indeed, all the consciousness or intelligence that manifests itself in the activities of life is but the reflection of the All-pervading, Absolute and Perfect Intelligence—the Supreme Spirit.

293 Whatever his life &c.: Whether he be engaged in prescribed or forbidden acts, he is not born again. For, the acts, the seeds of rebirth, of a knower of p. 302 Truth are burnt by the fire of knowledge, and thus cannot be effective causes to bring about births. In his case they are mere semblances of Karma; a burnt cloth, for instance, cannot serve the purposes of a cloth.

294 Not knowing thus: not able to know the Self described above, by one of the several methods as pointed out.

From others: Achâryas or spiritual teachers.

Regarding—following with Shraddhâ.

What they have heard, i.e., they solely depend upon the authority of others' instructions.

295 Union . . . Kshetrajna: The union of Kshetra and Kshetrajna, of the object and the subject, is of the nature of mutual Adhyâsa which consists in confounding them as well as their attributes with each other, owing to the absence of discrimination of their real nature. This false knowledge vanishes when one is able to separate Kshetra from Kshetrajna.

28. Since seeing the Lord equally existent everywhere, he injures not Self by self, and so goes to the highest Goal.[296]

29. He sees, who sees that all actions are done by Prakriti alone and that the Self is actionless.

30. When he sees the separate existence of all beings inherent in the One, and their expansion from That (One) alone, he then becomes Brahman.

31. Being without beginning and devoid of Gunas, this Supreme Self, immutable, O son of Kunti, though existing in the body neither acts nor is affected.[297]

32. As the all-pervading Akâsha, because of its subtlety, is not tainted, so the Self existent in the body everywhere is not tainted.

33. As the one sun illumines all this world, so does He who abides in the Kshetra, O descendant of Bharata, illumine the whole Kshetra.

34. They who thus with the eye of knowledge perceive the distinction between the Kshetra and the Kshetrajna, and also the emancipation from the Prakriti of beings, they go to the Supreme.[298]

FOURTEENTH CHAPTER
The Discrimination of the Three Gunas

The Blessed Lord said:

1. Again shall I tell thee that supreme knowledge which is above all knowledge, having known which all the Munis have attained to high

296 He injures . . . by self—like the ignorant man either by ignoring the Self in others (Avidyâ or nescience), or regarding the non-Self (physical body, &c.) as the Self (Mithyâ-jnâna or false knowledge)—the two veils that hide the true nature of the Self.

297 Being without beginning—having no cause.
Neither . . . affected—Because the Self is not the doer, therefore He is not touched by the fruit of action.

298 Prakriti of beings: the material nature or delusion of beings due to Avidyâ.

perfection after this life.[299]

2. They who having devoted themselves to this knowledge, have attained to My Being, are neither born at the time of creation, nor are they troubled at the time of dissolution.

3. My womb is the great Prakriti; in that I place the germ; from thence, O descendant of Bharata, is the birth of all beings.[300]

4. Whatever forms are produced, O son of Kunti, in all the wombs, the great Prakriti is their womb, and I the seed-giving Father.

5. Sattva, Rajas, and Tamas,—these Gunas, O mighty-armed, born of Prakriti, bind fast in the body the indestructible embodied one.[301]

6. Of these Sattva, from its stainlessness luminous and free from evil, binds, O sinless one, by attachment to happiness, and by attachment to knowledge.[302]

7. Know Rajas to be of the nature of passion, giving rise to thirst and attachment; it binds fast, O son of Kunti, the embodied one, by attachment to action.[303]

8. And know Tamas to be born of ignorance, stupefying all embodied beings; it binds fast, O descendant of Bharata, by miscomprehension, indolence, and sleep.[304]

---

299 After this life—after being freed from this bondage of the body.

300 Brahma: This word is derived from Brimh, 'to expand,' and means here the vast seed or womb (the Prakriti) out of which the cosmos is evolved or expanded.

I place the germ: I infuse the reflection of My Intelligence, and this act of impregnation is the cause of the evolution of the cosmos.

301 These Gunas—are the primary constituents of the Prakriti and are the bases of all substances; they cannot therefore be said to be attributes or qualities inhering in the substances as opposed to the substances.

Embodied one: he who abides in the body as if identified therewith.

302 Binds by attachment to happiness &c.: Binds the Self by the consciousness of happiness and knowledge in the shape of 'I am happy,' 'I am wise,' which belongs properly to the Kshetra, but which is associated with the Self, the Absolute Intelligence and Bliss, through Avidyâ.

303 It binds &c.—Though the Self is not the agent, Rajas makes Him act with the idea 'I am the doer.'

304 Stupefying: causing delusion or non-discrimination.

9. Sattva attaches to happiness, and Rajas to action, O descendant of Bharata; while Tamas, verily, shrouding discrimination, attaches to miscomprehension.

10. Sattva arises, O descendant of Bharata, predominating over Rajas and 'Tamas; and Rajas over Sattva and Tamas; so, Tamas over Sattva and Rajas.[305]

11. When through every sense in this body, the light of intelligence shines, then it should be known that Sattva is predominant.[306]

12. Greed, activity, the undertaking of actions, unrest, longing—these arise when Rajas is predominant, O bull of the: Bhâratas.[307]

13. Darkness, inertness, miscomprehension, and delusion,—these arise when Tamas is predominant, O descendant of Kuru.[308]

14. If the embodied one meets death when Sattva is predominant, then he attains to the spotless regions of the worshippers of the Highest. [309]

15. Meeting death in Rajas he is born among those attached to action; so dying in Tamas, he is born in the wombs of the irrational.[310]

16. The fruit of good action, they say, is Sâttvika and pure; verily, the fruit of Rajas is pain, and ignorance is the fruit of Tamas.[311]

17. From Sattva arises wisdom, and greed from Rajas; miscomprehension, delusion and ignorance arise from Tamas.

18. The Sattva-abiding go upwards; the Râjasika dwell in the middle; and the Tâmasika, abiding in the function. of the lowest Guna, go down-

305 When one or the other of the Gunas asserts itself predominating over the other two, it produces its own effect. Sattva produces knowledge and happiness; Rajas, action; Tamas, veiling of discrimination &c.

306 Every sense—lit., all the gates. All the senses are for the Self the gateways of perception.

307 Unrest—being agitated with joy, attachment &c.

308 Darkness, inertness: Absence of discrimination, and its results, inertness &c.

309 Spotless regions: The Brahma-loka and the like the Highest—Deities such as Hiranyagarbha.

310 Meeting . . . Rajas: If he dies when Rajas is predominant in him.

311 Rajas—means Râjasika action, and Tamas,—Tâmasika action, as this section treats of actions.

wards.

19. When the seer beholds no agent other than the Gunas and knows That which is higher than the Gunas, he attains to My being.[312]

20. The embodied one having gone beyond these three Gunas out of which the body is evolved, is freed from birth, death, decay and pain, and attains to immortality.

Arjuna said:

21. By what marks, O Lord, is he (known) who has gone beyond these three Gunas? What is his conduct, and how does he pass beyond these three Gunas?

The Blessed Lord said:

22. He who hates not the appearance of light, (the effect of Sattva), activity (the effect of Rajas), and delusion (the effect of Tamas), (in his own mind), O Pândava, nor longs for them when absent;[313]

23. He who, sitting like one unconcerned, is moved not by the Gunas, who, knowing that the Gunas operate, is Self-centred and swerves not;

24. Alike in pleasure and pain, Self-abiding, regarding a clod of earth, a stone and gold alike; the same to agreeable and disagreeable, firm, the same in censure and, praise;[314]

25. The same in honour and disgrace, the same to friend and foe, relinquishing all undertakings—he is said to have gone beyond the Gunas. [315]

---

312 The Gunas—which transform themselves into the bodies, senses and sense-objects, and which in all their modifications constitute the agent in all actions.
Knows . . . the Gunas: Sees Him who is distinct from the Gunas, who is the Witness of the Gunas and of their functions.

313 This answers Arjuna's first question. The man of right knowledge does not hate the effects of the three Gunas when they clearly present themselves as objects of consciousness; nor does he long after things which have disappeared.

314 Self-abiding: He remains in his own true-nature.

315 Inclining to neither of the dual throng, he firmly treads the path of Self-knowledge, and rises above the Gunas.
These three Slokas are in answer to Arjuna's second question.

26. And he who serves Me with an unswerving devotion, he, going beyond the Gunas, is fitted for becoming Brahman.[316]

27. For I am the abode of Brahman, the Immortal and Immutable, of everlasting Dharma and of Absolute Bliss.[317]

FIFTEENTH CHAPTER
The Way to the Supreme Spirit

The Blessed Lord said:

1. They speak of an eternal Ashvattha rooted above and branching below, whose leaves are the Vedas; he who knows it, is a Veda-knower.[318]

2. Below and above spread its branches, nourished by the Gunas; sense-objects are its buds; and below in the world of man stretch forth the roots, originating action.[319]

3-4. Its form is not here perceived as such, neither its end, nor its origin, nor its existence. Having cut asunder this firm-rooted Ashvattha with the strong axe of non-attachment,—then that Goal is to be sought for, going whither they (the wise) do not return again. I seek refuge in

---

316 This answers Arjuna's third question.

317 I—the Pratyagâtman, the true Inner-Self.

318 Ashvattha: literally, that which does not endure till to-morrow: the Samsâra, the ever-changing, phenomenal world.

Brahman with Its unmanifested energy Mâyâ, is spoken of as the One "above," for It is supreme over all things; the One above is the root of this Tree of Samsâra, as such it is said to have its root above. Mahat, Ahamkâra Tanmâtrâs, etc., are its branches evolving to grosser and grosser states—hence it is said to be branching "below." As leaves protect a tree, so do the Vedas protect the Tree of Samsâra, as treating of Dharma and Adharma, with their causes and fruits.

Eternal—because this Tree of Samsâra rests on a continuous series of births without beginning and end, and it cannot be cut down except by the knowledge, "I am Brahman."

319 Below: from man downwards.

Above: up to Brahmâ.

Roots: The tap-root is the Lord "above"; the p. 325 secondary roots are the Samskâras, attachment and aversion etc. It is these that, being in perpetual succession the cause and consequence of good and evil deeds, bind one fast to actions—Dharma and Adharma.

that Primeval Purusha whence streamed forth the Eternal Activity.[320]

5. Free from pride and delusion, with the evil of attachment conquered, ever dwelling in the Self, with desires completely receded, liberated from the pairs of opposites known as pleasure and pain, the undeluded reach that Goal Eternal.

6. That the sun illumines not, nor the moon, nor fire; that is My Supreme Abode, going whither they return not.

7. An eternal portion of Myself having become a living soul in the world of life, draws (to itself) the (five) senses with mind for the sixth, abiding in Prakriti.[321]

8. When the Lord obtains a body and when He leaves it, He takes these and goes, as the wind takes the scents from their seats (the flowers). [322]

9. Presiding over the ear, the eye, the touch, the taste and the smell, as also the mind, He experiences objects.

10. Him while transmigrating from one body to another, or residing (in the same) or experiencing, or when united with the Gunas,—the deluded do not see; but those who have the eye of wisdom behold Him.[323]

11. The Yogis striving (for perfection) behold Him dwelling in themselves; but the unrefined and unintelligent, even though striving,

---

320 As such: it cannot be said to exist, because it appears and vanishes every other moment. See commentary on II. 16.
Tat—That—Sankara and Anandagiri read 'Tatah,' and explain it as beyond or above the Ashvattha, the Tree of Samsâra.
The Eternal Activity: this ever-passing work of projection, this ever-flowing current of evolution, the world of phenomena.

321 The Jiva or the individual soul is that aspect of the Supreme Self which manifests itself in every one as the doer and enjoyer, being limited by the Upâdhis set up by Avidyâ; but in reality, both are the same. It is like the Akâsha (space) in the jar, which is a portion of the infinite Akâsha, and becomes one with the latter on the destruction of the jar, the cause of limitation.

322 Lord: Jiva spoken of in the preceding Sloka.
When the Jiva leaves the body, then he draws round himself the senses and the Manas. When he enters another he takes these again with him, i.e., he is born with these again.

323 Though Atman is nearest and comes most easily within the range of their consciousness in a variety of functions, still all do not see Him, because of their complete subservience to sense-objects.

see Him not.[324]

12. The light which, residing in the sun illumines the whole world, that which is in the moon and in the fire—know that light to be Mine.[325]

13. Entering the earth with My energy, I support all beings, and I nourish all the herbs, becoming the watery moon.[326]

14. Abiding in the body of living beings as (the fire) Vaishvânara, I, associated with Prâna and Apâna, digest the fourfold food.[327]

15. I am centred in the hearts of all; memory and perception as well as their loss come from Me. I am verily that which has to be known by all the Vedas, I indeed am the Author of the Vedânta, and the Knower of the Veda am I.[328]

16. There are two Purushas in the world,—the Perishable and the Imperishable. All beings are the Perishable; and the Kutastha is called Imperishable.[329]

324 The unrefined: Whose mind has not been regenerated by Tapas and subjugation of the senses, whose mind is not purified.

325 Light—may also be understood to mean the light of consciousness.

326 Energy—Ojas: The energy of the Ishvara, whereby the vast heaven and the earth are firmly held.
Nourish—by infusing sap into them.
The watery moon: The Soma, moon, is considered as the repository or the embodiment of all fluids (Rasas.)

327 See IV. 29.
Vaishvânara: The fire abiding in the stomach.
Fourfold food: Food which has to be eaten by (1) mastication, (2) sucking, (3) licking, and (4):swallowing.

328 Memory—of what is experienced in the past births; and knowledge—of things transcending the ordinary limits of space, time and visible nature.—Anandagiri.
Come from Me—as the result of their good or evil deeds.
I indeed . . . Vedânta: It is I who am the Teacher of the wisdom of the Vedanta, and cause it to be handed down in regular succession.

329 Two Purushas: Two categories—arranged in, two separate groups of beings,—spoken of as: 'Purushas,' as they are the Upâdhis of the Purusha.
Imperishable—Mâyâ-Sakti of the Lord, the germ from which the perishable being takes its birth.
Kutastha: That which manifests Itself in various forms of illusion and deception. It is said to be imperishable, as the seed of Samsâra is endless,—in the sense that it does not perish in the absence of Brahma-Jnâna.

17. But (there is) another, the Supreme Purusha, called the Highest Self, the immutable Lord, who pervading the three worlds, sustains them. [330]

18. As I transcend the Perishable and am above even the Imperishable, therefore am I in the world and in the Veda celebrated as the Purushottama, (the Highest Purusha).[331]

19. He who free from delusion thus knows Me, the Highest Spirit, he knowing all, worships Me with all his heart, O descendant of Bharata.

20. Thus, O sinless one, has this most profound teaching been imparted by Me. Knowing this one attains the highest intelligence and will have accomplished all one's duties, O descendant of Bharata.[332]

SIXTEENTH CHAPTER
The Classification of the Divine and the Non-Divine Attributes

The Blessed Lord said:

1. Fearlessness, purity of heart, steadfastness in knowledge and Yoga; almsgiving, control of the senses, Yajna, reading of the Shâstras, austerity, uprightness;[333]

2. Non-injury, truth, absence of anger, renunciation, tranquillity, absence of calumny, compassion to beings, un-covetousness, gentleness,

---

330 Another: quite distinct from the two.
The three Worlds: Bhuh (the Earth), Bhuvah (the Mid-Region) and Svah (the Heaven).

331 The Perishable—The Tree of Samsâra called Ashvattha.
The Imperishable—Which constitutes the seed of the Tree of Samsâra.

332 Highest intelligence—which realises the Brahman.
Will have accomplished . . . duties: Whatever duty one has to do in life, all that duty has been done, when the Brahman is realised.

333 Yoga—consists in making what has been learnt from the Shâstras and the Achârya an object of one's own direct perception, by concentration and self-control.

modesty, absence of fickleness;[334]

3. Boldness, forgiveness, fortitude, purity, absence of hatred, absence of pride; these belong to one born for a divine state, O descendant of Bharata.

4. Ostentation, arrogance and self-conceit, anger as also harshness and ignorance, belong to one who is born, O Pârtha, for an Asurika state.[335]

5. The divine state is deemed to make for liberation, the Asurika for bondage; grieve not, O Pândava, thou art born for a divine state.

6. There are two types of beings in this world, the divine and the Asurika. The divine have been described at length; hear from Me, O Pârtha, of the Asurika.

7. The persons of Asurika nature know not what to do and what to refrain from; neither is purity found in them nor good conduct, nor truth.[336]

8. They say, "The universe is without truth, without a (moral) basis, without a God, brought about by mutual union, with lust for its cause; what else?"[337]

9. Holding this view, these ruined souls of small intellect and fierce deeds, rise as the enemies of the world for its destruction.[338]

10. Filled with insatiable desires, full of hypocrisy, pride and arrogance, holding evil ideas through delusion, they work with impure resolve.

11. Beset with immense cares ending only with death, regarding

334 Uncovetousness: Unaffectedness of the senses when in contact with their objects.
Absence of fickleness: Avoidance of useless actions.—Sridhara.

335 Asurika: demoniac.

336 What to do . . . from: What acts they should perform to achieve the end of man, nor what acts they should abstain from to avert evil.

337 Without truth: As we are unreal so this universe is unreal, and the sacred Scriptures that declare the truth are unreal.
What else—but lust can be the cause of the universe?—This is the view of the Lokâyatikas, the materialists.

338 Small intellect—as it concerns itself only with sense-objects and cannot soar higher.

gratification of lust as the highest, and feeling sure that that is all;[339]

12. Bound by a hundred ties of hope, given over to lust and wrath, they strive to secure by unjust means hoards of wealth for sensual enjoyment.

13. "This to-day has been gained by me; this desire I shall obtain; this is mine, and this wealth also shall be mine in future.

14. "That enemy has been slain by me, and others also shall I slay. I am the lord, I enjoy, I am successful, powerful and happy.

15. "I am rich and well-born. Who else is equal to me? I will sacrifice, I will give, I will rejoice." Thus deluded by ignorance,

16. Bewildered by many a fancy, covered by the meshes of delusion, addicted to the gratification of lust, they fall down into a foul hell.

17. Self-conceited, haughty, filled with the pride and intoxication of wealth, they perform sacrifices in name, out of ostentation, disregarding ordinance;

18. Possessed of egoism, power, insolence, lust and wrath, these malignant people hate Me (the Self within) in their own bodies and those of others.

19. These malicious and cruel evildoers, most degraded of men, I hurl perpetually into the wombs of Asuras only, in these worlds.[340]

20. Obtaining the Asurika wombs, and deluded birth after birth, not attaining to Me, they thus fall, O son of Kunti, into a still lower condition.

21. Triple is this gate of hell, destructive of the self,—lust, anger and greed; therefore one should forsake these three.[341]

22. The man who has got beyond these three gates of darkness, O son of Kunti, practises what is good for himself, and thus goes to the Goal Supreme.

339 Cares—as to the means of acquiring and preserving the innumerable objects of desire.

340 Wombs of Asuras: Wombs of the most cruel beings, as tigers, snakes, etc.

Worlds: Paths of Samsâra passing through many a hell.

341 Destructive of the self: making the self fit for no human end whatever.

23. He who, setting aside the ordinance of the Shâstra, acts under the impulse of desire, attains not to perfection, nor happiness, nor the Goal Supreme.[342]

24. So let the Shâstra be thy authority in ascertaining what ought to be done and what ought not to be done. Having known what is said in the ordinance of the Shâstra, thou shouldst act here.[343]

SEVENTEENTH CHAPTER
The Enquiry into the Threefold Shraddha

Arjuna said:

1. Those who setting aside the ordinance of the Shâstra, perform sacrifice with Shraddhâ, what is their condition, O Krishna? (Is it) Sattva, Rajas or Tamas?[344]

The Blessed Lord said:

2. Threefold is the Shraddhâ of the embodied, which is inherent in their nature,—the Sâttvika, the Râjasika and the Tâmasika. Do thou hear of it.[345]

3. The Shraddhâ of each is according to his natural disposition, O descendant of Bharata. The man consists of his Shraddhâ; he verily is what his Shraddhâ is.[346]

4. Sâttvika men worship the Devas; Râjasika, the Yakshas and the Râkshasas; the others—the Tâmasika men—the Pretas and the hosts of Bhutas.

5-6. Those men who practise severe austerities not enjoined by the

---

342 Perfection: fitness for attaining the end of man.

343 Here: in this world.

344 Setting . . . Shraddhâ: not that they believe the ordinance of the Shâstra to be false, but out of laziness or because of the difficulty in adhering to p. 350 them strictly, they let them alone and worship the gods, endued with Shraddhâ.

345 Inherent . . . nature: born of their past Samskâras. It—the threefold Shraddhâ.

346 Natural disposition—the specific tendencies or Samskâras.

Shâstras, given to ostentation and egoism, possessed with the power of lust and attachment, torture, senseless as they are, all the organs in the body, and Me dwelling in the body within; know them to be of Asurika resolve. [347]

7. The food also which is liked by each of them is threefold, as also Yajna, austerity and almsgiving. Do thou hear this, their distinction.

8. The foods which augment vitality, energy, strength, health, cheerfulness and appetite, which are savoury and oleaginous, substantial and agreeable, are liked by the Sâttvika.

9. The foods that are bitter, sour, saline, excessively hot, pungent, dry and burning, are liked by the Râjasika, and are productive of pain, grief and disease.[348]

10. That which is stale, tasteless, stinking, cooked overnight, refuse and impure, is the food liked by the Tâmasika.[349]

11. That Yajna is Sâttvika which is performed by men desiring no fruit, as enjoined by ordinance, with their mind fixed on the Yajna only, for its own sake.

12. That which is performed, O best of the Bhâratas, seeking for fruit and for ostentation, know it to be a Râjasika Yajna.

13. The Yajna performed without heed to ordinance, in which no food is distributed, which is devoid of Mantras, gifts, and Shraddhâ, is said to be Tâmasika.

14. Worship of the Devas, the twice-born, the Gurus and the wise, purity, straightforwardness, continence, and non-injury are called the austerity of the body.

15. Speech which causes no vexation, and is true, as also agreeable

347 Austerities—which cause pain to himself and to other living beings. Possessed attachment—may also be interpreted as, 'possessed of lust, attachment and power.'
All the organs of the body: the aggregate of all the elements composing the body.

348 Excessively—this word should be construed with each of the seven; thus, excessively bitter, excessively sour, and so on.

349 Stale—Yâtayâmam—lit. cooked three hours ago.
Refuse: left on the plate after a meal.

and beneficial, and regular study of the Vedas,—these are said to form the austerity of speech.[350]

16. Serenity of mind, kindliness, silence, self-control, honesty of motive,—this is called the mental austerity.[351]

17. This threefold austerity practised by steadfast men, with great Shraddhâ, desiring no fruit, is said to be Sâttvika.[352]

18. That austerity which is practised with the object of gaining welcome, honour and worship, and with ostentation, is here said to be Râjasika, unstable and transitory.[353]

19. That austerity which is practised out of a foolish notion, with self-torture or for the purpose of wining another, is declared to be Tâmasika.

20. To give is right, gift given with this idea, to one who does no service in return, in a fit place and to a worthy person, that gift is held to be Sâttvika.[354]

21. And what is given with a view to receiving in return, or looking for the fruit, or again reluctantly, that gift is held to be Râjasika.

22. The gift that is given at the wrong place or time, to unworthy persons, without regard or with disdain, that is declared to be Tâmasika.

23. "Om, Tat, Sat": this has been declared to be the triple designation of Brahman. By that were made of old the Brâhmanas, the Vedas and the Yajnas.[355]

350 Speech, to be an austerity, must form an invariable combination of all the four attributes mentioned in the Sloka; if it lacks in one or other of them, it will no longer be an austerity of speech.

351 Silence—Maunam—is the result of the control of thought so far as it concerns speech. Or it may mean, the condition of the Muni, i.e., practice of meditation.

352 Steadfast—unaffected in success and failure.

353 With ostentation: for mere show, hypocritically, with no sincere belief.

Here—is explained also in the sense of 'of this world,' i.e., yielding fruit only in this world.

354 Who . . . return: one who cannot, or who though able is not expected to return the good.

355 Om, Tat, Sat: Om is the principal name of the Lord, because it means all that is manifest and the beyond. It also means "Yes." Tat means "That"; the

24. Therefore, uttering 'Om,' are the acts of sacrifice, gift and austerity as enjoined in the ordinances, always begun by the followers of the Vedas.

25. Uttering Tat, without aiming at fruits, are the various acts of Yajna, austerity and gift performed by the seekers of Moksha.

26. The word Sat is used in the sense of reality and of goodness; and so also, Pârtha, the word Sat is used in the sense of an auspicious act.

27. Steadiness in Yajna, austerity and gift is also called 'Sat': as also action in connection with these (or, action for the sake of the Lord) is called Sat.

28. Whatever is sacrificed, given or performed, and whatever austerity is practised without Shraddhâ, it is called Asat, O Pârtha; it is naught here or hereafter.[356]

EIGHTEENTH CHAPTER
The Way of Liberation in Renunciation

Arjuna said:

1. I desire to know severally, O mighty-armed, the truth of Sannyâsa, O Hrishikesha, as also of Tyâga, O slayer of Keshi.[357]

The Blessed Lord said:

2. The renunciation of Kâmya actions, the sages understand as. Sannyâsa: the wise declare the abandonment of the fruits of all works as Tyâga. [358]

3. Some philosophers declare that all action should be relinquished as an evil, whilst others (say) that the work of Yajna, gift and austerity

---

Indefinable, that which can only be described indirectly as "That which." Sat means Reality; which is ever permanent in one mode of being.

356 It is naught here or hereafter: Though costing much trouble it is of no use here as it is not acceptable to the wise ones, nor can it produce any effect conducive to good hereafter.

357 Sannyâsa and Tyâga both mean renunciation. Keshi—was an Asura.

358 Kâmya—which are accompanied with a desire for fruits.

should not be relinquished.

4. Hear from Me the final truth about relinquishment, O best of the Bhâratas. For relinquishment has been declared to be of three kinds, O tiger among men.

5. The work of Yajna, gift and austerity should not be relinquished, but it should indeed be performed; (for) Yajna, gift and austerity are purifying to the wise.

6. But even these works, O Pârtha, should be performed, leaving attachment and the fruits;—such is My best and certain conviction.

7. But the renunciation of obligatory action is not proper. Abandonment of the same from delusion is declared to be Tâmasika.[359]

8. He who from fear of bodily trouble relinquishes action, because it is painful, thus performing a Râjasika relinquishment, he obtains not the fruit thereof.[360]

9. When obligatory work is performed, O Arjuna, only because it ought to be done, leaving attachment and fruit, such relinquishment is regarded as Sâttvika.

10. The relinquisher endued with Sattva and a steady understanding and with his doubts dispelled, hates not a disagreeable work nor is attached to an agreeable one.

11. Actions cannot be entirely relinquished by an embodied being, but he who relinquishes the fruits of action is called a relinquisher.

12. The threefold fruit of action—disagreeable, agreeable and mixed,—accrues to non-relinquishers after death, but never to relinquishers.

13. Learn from Me, O mighty-armed, these five causes for the accomplishment of all works as declared in the wisdom which is the end of all action:[361]

14. The body, the agent, the various senses, the different functions of

359 Since it is purifying in the case of the ignorant.

360 Fruit, i.e., Moksha, which comes out of the renunciation of all actions accompanied with wisdom.

361 Wisdom: Sânkhya,—literally, in which all the things that are to be known are expounded, therefore, the highest wisdom.

a manifold kind, and the presiding divinity, the fifth of these;[362]

15. Whatever action a man performs by his body, speech and mind—whether right or the reverse—these five are its causes.

16. Such being the case, he who through a non-purified understanding looks upon his Self, the Absolute, as the agent, he of perverted mind sees not.

17. He who is free from the notion of egoism, whose intelligence is not affected (by good or evil), though he kills these people, he kills not, nor is bound (by the action);[363]

18. Knowledge, the known and the knower form the threefold cause of action. The instrument, the object and the agent are the threefold basis of action.[364]

19. Knowledge, action and agent are declared in the Sânkhya philosophy to be of three kinds only, from the distinction of Gunas: hear them also duly.[365]

20. That by which the one indestructible Substance is seen in all beings, inseparate in the separated, know that knowledge to be Sâttvika.[366]

21. But that knowledge which sees in all beings various entities of distinct kinds as different from one another, know thou that knowledge as Râjasika.[367]

---

362 Presiding divinity: Each of the senses has its god who presides over it, and by whose aid it discharges its own functions; e.g., the Aditya (Sun) is the presiding divinity of the eye, by whose aid it sees and acts; and so on with the other senses.

363 He whose self-consciousness, by the force of long, strenuous, and properly-trained self-concentration, is ever identified with Brahman, and not with the five causes of action as mentioned in Sloka 14,—he whose self-consciousness never mistakes itself for the body, mind and the like, even when performing physical acts,—he is ever free from the taint of action.

364 Basis—because the threefold action inheres in these three.

365 Sânkhya: the Science of the Gunas by Kapila. Though there is a conflict in the matter of supreme Truth—the oneness or non-duality of Brahman—between the Vedânta and the Sânkhya, yet the Sânkhya view is given here, because it is an authority on the science of Gunas.

Duly—described according to the Science, according to reason.

366 Inseparate: undifferentiated; permeating all.

367 Entities: Souls.

22. Whilst that which is confined to one single effect as if it were the whole, without reason, without foundation in truth, and trivial,—that is declared to be Tâmasika.[368]

23. An ordained action done without love or hatred by one not desirous of the fruit and free from attachment, is declared to be Sâttvika.

24. But the action which is performed desiring desires, or with self-conceit and with much effort, is declared to be Râjasika.

25. That action is declared to be Tâmasika which is undertaken through delusion, without heed to the consequence, loss (of power and wealth), injury (to others) and (one's own) ability.

26. An agent who is free from attachment, non-egotistic, endued with fortitude and enthusiasm and unaffected in success or failure, is called Sâttvika.

27. He who is passionate, desirous of the fruits of action, greedy, malignant, impure, easily elated or dejected, such an agent is called Râjasika.[369]

28. Unsteady, vulgar, arrogant, dishonest, malicious, indolent, desponding and procrastinating, such an agent is called Tâmasika.

29. Hear thou the triple distinction of intellect and fortitude, according to the Gunas, as I declare them exhaustively and severally, O Dhananjaya.[370]

30. That which knows the paths of work and renunciation, right and wrong action, fear and fearlessness, bondage and liberation, that intellect, O Pârtha, is Sâttvika.[371]

31. That which has a distorted apprehension of Dharma and its opposite and also of right action and its opposite, that intellect, O Pârtha,

Different from one another: Different in different bodies.

368 One single effect: such as the body,—thinking it to be the Self.

369 Elated or dejected—at the success or failure of the action in which he is engaged.

370 Dhananjaya: the conqueror of wealth—human and divine, earthly and celestial; an epithet of Arjuna.

371 Fear . . . liberation—the cause of fear and the cause of fearlessness; similarly, the cause of bondage and the cause of liberation.

is Râjasika.

32. That which enveloped in darkness regards Adharma as Dharma and views all things in a perverted light, that intellect, O Pârtha, is Tâmasika.

33. The fortitude by which the functions of the mind, the Prâna and the senses, O Pârtha, are regulated, that fortitude, unswerving through Yoga, is Sâttvika.

34. But the fortitude by which one regulates (one's mind) to Dharma, desire and wealth, desirous of the fruit of each from attachment, that fortitude, O Pârtha, is Râjasika.

35. That by which a stupid man does not give up sleep, fear, grief, despondency and also overweening conceit, that fortitude, O Pârtha, is Tâmasika.[372]

36. And now hear from Me, O bull of the Bhâratas, of the threefold happiness. That happiness which one learns to enjoy by habit, and by which one comes to the end of pain;

37. That which is like poison at first, but like nectar at the end; that happiness is declared to be Sâttvika, born of the translucence of intellect due to Self-realisation.

38. That which arises from the contact of object with sense, at first like nectar, but at the end like poison, that happiness is declared to be Râjasika. [373]

39. That happiness which begins and results in self-delusion arising from sleep, indolence and miscomprehension, that is declared to be Tâmasika.

40. There is no entity on earth, or again in heaven among the Devas, that is devoid of these three Gunas, born of Prakriti.

41. Of Brâhmanas and Kshatriyas and Vaishyas, as also of Sudras, O scorcher of foes, the duties are distributed according to the Gunas born

---

372 Does not give up sleep &c.,—is inordinately addicted to sleep &c., regarding these to be only proper.

373 At the end like poison—because it leads to deterioration in strength, vigour, complexion, wisdom, intellect, wealth and energy.

of their own nature.[374]

42. The control of the mind and the senses, austerity, purity, forbearance, and also uprightness, knowledge, realisation, belief in a hereafter,—these are the duties of the Brâhmanas, born of (their own) nature.

43. Prowess, boldness, fortitude, dexterity, and also not flying from battle, generosity and sovereignty are the duties of the Kshatriyas, born of (their own) nature.

44. Agriculture, cattle-rearing and trade are the duties of the Vaishyas, born of (their own) nature; and action consisting of service is the duty of the Sudras, born of (their own) nature.

45. Devoted each to his own duty, man attains the highest perfection. How engaged in his own duty, he attains perfection, that hear.[375]

46. From whom is the evolution of all beings, by whom all this is pervaded, worshipping Him with his own duty, a man attains perfection. [376]

47. Better is one's own Dharma, (though) imperfect, than the Dharma of another well-performed. He who does the duty ordained by his own nature incurs no evil.[377]

48. One should not relinquish, O son of Kunti, the duty to which one is born, though it is attended with evil; for, all undertakings are enveloped

---

374 According to the Karma or habits and tendencies formed by desire, action and association in the past life manifesting themselves in the present as effects. Or, nature (Svabhâva) may here mean the Mâyâ made up of the three Gunas, the Prakriti of the Lord.

375 Own—according to his nature.
The Apastamba Dharma-Shâstra says: "Men of several castes and orders, each devoted to his respective duties, reap the fruits of their actions after death, and then by the residual Karma attain to births in superior countries, castes and families, possessed of comparatively superior Dharma, span of life, learning, conduct, wealth, happiness and intelligence."

376 The highest worship to the Lord consists in the closest approach to Him. The veil of Mâyâ comprising Karma or habits, tendencies and actions prevents a man from nearing the Lord, i.e., realising his own Self. By working out one's Karma alone, according to the law of one's being, can this veil be rent and the end accomplished.

377 As a poisonous substance does not injure the worm born in that substance, so he who does his Svadharma incurs no evil.

by evil, as fire by smoke.[378]

49. He whose intellect is unattached everywhere, who has subdued his heart, whose desires have fled, he attains by renunciation to the supreme perfection, consisting of freedom from action.[379]

50. Learn from Me in brief, O son of Kunti, how reaching such perfection, he attains to Brahman, that supreme consummation of knowledge.

51. Endued with a pure intellect, subduing the body and the senses with fortitude, relinquishing sound and such other sense-objects, abandoning attraction and hatred;[380]

52. Resorting to a sequestered spot, eating but little, body, speech and mind controlled, ever engaged in meditation and concentration, possessed of dispassion;[381]

53. Forsaking egoism, power, pride, lust, wrath and property, freed from the notion of "mine," and tranquil, he is fit for becoming Brahman. [382]

378 Duty etc.—this need not mean caste duty.
All undertakings: one's own as well as others' duties.
The greatest evil is bondage and this endures so long as one lives in the realm of the Gunas, except in the case of a freed soul. All action is comprised in one or the other of the Gunas. All action therefore involves the evil of bondage.

379 He attains . . . renunciation—This may also be interpreted to mean: he attains the supreme state in which he remains as the actionless Self, by his renunciation of all actions, for which he is prepared by his right knowledge.

380 Pure: free from doubt and misconception, being merged in Brahman through the elimination of all alien attributes ascribed to It.
Relinquishing sound &c.—abandoning all superfluous luxuries, all objects except those only which are necessary for the bare maintenance of the body, and laying aside attraction and hatred even for those objects.

381 Eating but little—as conducive to the serenity of thought by keeping off languor, sleepiness and the like.
Meditation—upon the nature of the Self.
Concentration—one-pointedness of thought, on one feature of the Self.
Dispassion—for the seen and the unseen.

382 Power—that power which is combined with passion and desire.
Property: Though a man who is free from all passions of the mind and the senses, may own so much of external belongings as is necessary for bodily sustenance and for the observance of his religious duties (Dharma), yet this the aspirant abandons, even if this comes of itself, because he does not regard the bodily life as his; thus he becomes a Paramahamsa Parivrâjaka, a Sannyâsin of the highest order.

54. Brahman-become, tranquil-minded, he neither grieves nor desires; the same to all beings, he attains to supreme devotion unto Me. [383]

55. By devotion he knows Me in reality, what and who I am; then having known Me in reality, he forthwith enters into Me.

56. Even doing all actions always, taking refuge in Me,—by My grace he attains to the eternal, immutable State.

57. Resigning mentally all deeds to Me, having Me as the highest goal, resorting to Buddhi-Yoga do thou ever fix thy mind on Me.

58. Fixing thy mind on Me, thou shalt, by My grace, overcome all obstacles; but if from self-conceit thou wilt not hear Me, thou shalt perish.

59. If filled with self-conceit thou thinkest, "I will not fight," vain is this thy resolve; thy Prakriti will constrain thee.[384]

60. Fettered, O son of Kunti, by thy own Karma, born of thy own nature, what thou, from delusion, desirest not to do, thou shalt have to do in spite of thyself.

61. The Lord, O Arjuna, dwells in the hearts of all beings, causing all beings, by His Mâyâ, to revolve, (as if) mounted on a machine.[385]

62. Take refuge in Him with all thy heart, O Bhârata; by His grace shalt thou attain supreme peace (and) the eternal abode.

63. Thus has wisdom more profound than all profundities, been declared to. thee by Me; reflecting over it fully, act as thou likest.[386]

64. Hear thou again My supreme word, the profoundest of all; because thou art dearly beloved of Me, therefore will I speak what is good to thee. [387]

---

383 Brahman-become: not that he is yet freed and become the Absolute, but is firmly grounded in the knowledge that he is Brahman. His attainment of freedom is described in the next verse.

Supreme devotion: the devotion stated in VII. 17.

384 Thy Prakriti: Thy nature as a Kshatriya.

385 See commentary to IX. 10.

Arjuna means 'white,' and here it signifies—'O pure-hearted one.'

386 It: the Shâstra, the teaching as declared above.

387 Again: though more than once declared.

65. Occupy thy mind with Me, be devoted to Me, sacrifice to Me, bow down to Me. Thou shalt reach Myself; truly do I promise unto thee, (for) thou art dear to Me.[388]

66. Relinquishing all Dharmas take refuge in Me alone; I will liberate thee from all sins; grieve not.[389]

67. This is never to be spoken by thee to one who is devoid of austerities or devotion, nor to one who does not render service, nor to one who cavils at Me.[390]

68. He who with supreme devotion to Me will teach this deeply profound philosophy to My devotees, shall doubtless come to Me alone. [391]

69. Nor among men is there any who does dearer service to Me, nor shall there be another on earth dearer to Me, than he.[392]

70. And he who will study this sacred dialogue of ours, by him shall I have been worshipped by the Yajna of knowledge; such is My convic-

388 Thou shalt reach Myself: Thus acting,—i.e., looking upon the Lord alone as thy aim, means and end—thou shalt attain the Highest.
Truly do I promise unto thee.—Have implicit faith in the declarations of Me, the Lord, as I pledge thee My troth.

389 All Dharmas—including Adharma also: all actions, righteous or unrighteous, since absolute freedom from the bondage of all action is intended to be taught here.
Take refuge in Me alone—knowing that there is naught else except Me, the Self of all, dwelling the same in all.
Liberate thee—by manifesting Myself as thy own Self.
All sins: all bonds of Dharma and Adharma.
Sankara in his commentary here very strongly combats the opinion of those who hold that highest spiritual realisation (Jnâna) and ritualistic work (Karma) may go together in the same person. For Karma is possible only in the relative world (Samsâra), which is the outcome of ignorance; and knowledge dispels this ignorance. So neither the conjunction of Jnâna with Karma, nor Karma alone conduces to the absolute cessation of Samsâra, but it is only the Right Knowledge of the Self which does so.

390 This—Shâstra which has been taught to you.
Service—to the Guru; also means,—to one who does not wish to hear.

391 Teach—in the faith that he is thus doing service to the Lord, the Supreme Teacher.
Doubtless: or, freed from doubts.

392 He: who hands down the Shâstra to a fit person.

tion. [393]

71. And even that man who hears this, full of Shraddhâ and free from malice, he too, liberated, shall attain to the happy worlds of those of righteous deeds.[394]

72. Has this been heard by thee, Pârtha, with an attentive mind? Has the delusion of thy ignorance been destroyed, O Dhananjaya?

Arjuna said:

73. Destroyed is my delusion, and I have gained my memory through Thy grace, O Achyuta. I am firm; my doubts are gone. I will do Thy word. [395]

Sanjaya said:

74. Thus have I heard this wonderful dialogue between Vâsudeva and the high-souled Pârtha, causing my hair to stand on end.

75. Through the grace of Vyâsa have I heard this supreme and most profound Yoga, direct from Krishna, the Lord of Yoga, Himself declaring it.[396]

76. O King, as I remember and remember this wonderful and holy dialogue between Keshava and Arjuna, I rejoice again and again.[397]

77. And as I remember and remember that most wonderful Form of Hari, great is my wonder, O King; and I rejoice again and again.[398]

---

393 Yajna of knowledge: A Yajna can be performed in four ways, such as (1) Vidhi or ritual, (2). Japa, (3) Upâmsu, or a prayer uttered, in a low voice, or (4) Mânasa or prayer offered with the mind. Jnâna-yajna or the Yajna of knowledge comes under the head of Mânasa, and is therefore the highest.
The study of the Gitâ will produce an effect equal to that of the Yajna of knowledge.

394 Even that man: much more so he who understands the doctrine.

395 Memory—of the true nature of the Self.
Firm—in Thy command.
The purpose of the knowledge of the Shâstras is the destruction of doubts and delusions, and the recognition of the true nature of the Self. Here, the answer of Arjuna conclusively shows, that that purpose has been fulfilled in him.

396 Through . . . Vyâsa: by obtaining from him the Divya-chakshu or divine vision.

397 King: Dhritarâshtra.

398 Form: Vishvarupa, the Universal Form.

78. Wherever is Krishna, the Lord of Yoga, wherever is Pârtha, the wielder of the bow, there are prosperity, victory, expansion, and sound policy: such is my conviction.[399]

THE GREATNESS OF THE GITA

Salutation to Sri Ganesha!

Salutation to Sri Râdhâramana![400]

Dharâ (the Earth) said:

1. O Blessed Lord, O Supreme Ruler, how may one, who is held back by his Prârabdha Karma, obtain unswerving devotion?[401]

The Lord Vishnu said:

2. If one be devoted to the constant practice of the Gita, even though he be restrained by Prârabdha Karma, yet is he Mukta, happy, in this very world. lie is not tainted by (new) Karma.

3. No evil, however great, can affect him who meditates on the Gita. He is like the lotus leaf untouched by the water.

4-5. Where there is the book of the Gita, where its study is proceeded with, there are present all the holy places, there verily, are Prayâga and the rest. There also are all the Devas, Rishis, Yogins, and Pannagas, so also the Gopâlas and Gopikâs, with Nârada, Uddhava and their whole train of comrades.

399 The bow—called the Gândiva.

400 Ganesha is the god of wisdom and remover of obstacles; hence he is invoked and worshipped at the commencement of every important undertaking. Râdhâramana—the Lover of Râdhâ,—Sri Krishna.

401 Prârabdha Karma—There are three kinds of Karma: (1) Sanchita or accumulated and stored up in past lives; (2) Agâmi or that which is yet to be done; (3) Prârabdha or that which is already bearing fruit. This last is that part of the accumulated actions (Sanchita) which has brought about the present life and will influence it until its close. The knowledge of Brahman destroys all accumulated Karma and makes the current work abortive. But the Prârabdha Karma must run out its course, though the balanced mind of a liberated man is not affected by it.

6. Where the Gita is read, forthwith comes help. Where the Gita is discussed, recited, taught, or heard, there, O Earth, beyond a doubt, do I Myself unfailingly reside.

7. In the refuge of the Gita I abide; the Gita is My chief abode. Standing on the wisdom of the Gita, I maintain the three worlds.

8-9. The Gita is My Supreme Knowledge; it is undoubtedly inseparable from Brahman, this Knowledge is absolute, imperishable, eternal, of the essence of My inexpressible State, the Knowledge comprising the whole of the three Vedas, supremely blissful and consisting of the realisation of the true nature of the Self,—declared by the All-knowing and Blessed Krishna, through his own lips, to Arjuna.[402]

10. That man who with steady mind recites the eighteen chapters daily, attains the perfection of knowledge and thus reaches the highest plane.

11. If the whole cannot be recited, then half of it may be read; and he who does this acquires merit, equal to that of the gift of a cow. There is no doubt about. this.

12. By the recitation of a third part,. he gains the same merit as by bathing in the Ganges. By the repetition of a. sixth part, he obtains the fruit of the Soma-sacrifice.

13. He who reads, full of devotion, even one chapter daily, attains to the Rudraloka, and lives there for a long time, having become one of those who wait on Shiva.[403]

14. The man who daily reads a quarter of a chapter, or of a Sloka, O Earth, attains to human birth throughout the duration of a Manu.[404]

15-16. The man who recites ten, seven, five, four, three or two Slokas, or even one or half a Sloka of the Gita, certainly lives in Chandraloka for ten thousand years. He who leaves the body while reading the Gita, obtains the world of Man.

17. Again practising the Gita, he attains Supreme Mukti. The dying

402 Ardhamâtrâ—lit. the half-syllable, and refers to the dot on the ; symbolically, it stands for the Turiya state, hence the Absolute.

403 Become &c.—lit., attained to Ganahood.

404 Attains to Manhood: is born every time in a man-body.

man uttering the word "Gita" will attain the goal.

18. One who loves to hear the meaning of the Gita, even though he has committed heinous sins, attains to heaven, and lives in beatitude with Vishnu.

19. He who constantly meditates on the meaning of the Gita, even though he performs Karma incessantly, he is to be regarded as a Jivan-mukta, and after the destruction of his body he attains to the highest plane of knowledge.

20. By the help of this Gita, many kings like Janaka became free from their impurities and attained to the highest goal. It is so sung.

21. He who having finished the reading of the Gita, does not read its Mâhâtmyam as declared here, his reading is in vain, it is all labour wasted.

22. He who studies the Gita, accompanied with this discourse on its Mâhâtmyam, obtains the fruit stated herein, and reaches that goal which is difficult to attain.

Suta said:

23. He who will read this eternal greatness of the Gita, declared by me, after having finished the reading of the Gita itself, will obtain the fruit described herein.[405]

---

405 These declarations will, no doubt, seem to be mere flights of extravagant fancy, if they are taken in their literal sense. They may be explained either (1) as mere Arthavâda or a statement of glorification meant to stimulate a strong desire for the study of the Gita, which being performed from day to day, may, by the force of the truth and grandeur of one or other of its teachings, strike an inner chord of the heart some time, so much so as to change the whole nature of the man for good; (2) or, the "reading" and "reciting" and so forth, of the whole or a part, may not perhaps be taken in their ordinary sense, as meaning lip-utterance and the like, but in view of the great results indicated, they may be reasonably construed to mean the assimilation of the essence of the Gita teachings into the practical daily life of the individual. What wonder, then, that such a one who is the embodiment of the Gita would be a true Jnânin, or a Jivanmukta, or that he would, in proportion to his success of being so, attain the intermediate spheres of evolution and finally obtain Mukti?

Endnote

Upādhi is a profound concept in Indian philosophy, especially within Vedanta, and is often mentioned in commentaries on texts like the Bhagavad Gita and Upanishads.

Upādhi literally means "limiting adjunct" or "external condition". It refers to any attribute, condition, or limiting factor that causes the infinite Self (Ātman or Brahman) to appear as finite or limited.

Simple Analogy

Think of space and a pot:

Space is everywhere and infinite.

When you place a pot in space, it seems as if the pot "contains" a small space inside it.

That limited space is not really separate from the infinite space — it's just limited by the pot.

In this analogy:

Space = Brahman (infinite Self)

Pot = Upādhi

Pot-space = the individual self (jīva), seemingly limited

Mâhâtmyam "Māhātmyam" refers to the divine glory or exalted qualities of a deity, text, or sacred place.

www.ingramcontent.com/pod-product-compliance
Lightning Source LLC
Chambersburg PA
CBHW070833100426
42813CB00003B/601

* 9 7 8 1 9 6 8 1 9 4 1 0 9 *